Advanced Word Problems
(including Quantitative Review)

Chad Troutwine · Markus Moberg · Chris Kane · Mark Glenn

Co-Founders	**Chad Troutwine**
	Markus Moberg
Managing Editor	**Mark Glenn**
Director of Academic Programs	**Brian Galvin**
Interior Design	**Miriam Lubow**
	Lisa Johnson
Cover Design	**Nick Mason**
	Mike Miller
Contributing Editors	**Jim Stekelberg**
	Tatiana Becker
	Lissette Padilla
	Jeff Lev
Contributing Writers	**Adam Groden**
	Jim Stekelberg

A successful educational program is only as good as the people who teach it, and Veritas Prep is fortunate to have many of the world's finest GMAT instructors on its team.

Not only does that team know how to teach a strong curriculum, but it also knows how to help create one. This lesson book would not be possible without the hundreds of suggestions we have received from our talented faculty all across the world—from Seattle, Detroit, and Miami to London, Singapore, and Dubai. Their passion for excellence helped give birth to a new curriculum that is far better than what we could have created on our own.

Our students also deserve a very special thanks. Thousands of them have provided us with something priceless: enthusiastic feedback that has guided us in creating the most comprehensive GMAT preparation course available on the market today.

We therefore dedicate this revised lesson book to all Veritas Prep instructors and students who have tackled the GMAT and given us their valuable input along the way.

Table of Contents

Lesson 14 Introduction

Though the amount of math material tested on the GMAT may appear to be overwhelming, in essence, it all goes back to a limited set of key concepts. Even the most convoluted word problems rely on this principle. Today we will examine ways to break down tricky problems into their underlying concepts. We will also review these key concepts through a series of questions that highlight the most important aspects of the Quantitative portion of the exam. Your Veritas instructor will lead you through these questions, tying together all of the information you've learned over the past several lessons so that you can approach every problem on the real test with a high degree of confidence. We will also give you some of our best, tried and true last-minute tips for doing well on test day.

Advanced Word Problems

Quant questions often appear in the form of word problems. Test-takers generally perform poorly on these lengthier questions, so the makers of the GMAT typically classify word problems as difficult. In fact, the mathematical operations required to solve word problems are sometimes easier than their pared down siblings. One can conclude that the extra verbiage in word problems intimidates some test-takers. Other students may simply get bogged down or confused. In this section we will examine some of the more difficult types of word problems and hone the strategies for approaching them.

Approach the problem in steps using simple language

One of the keys to performing well on a difficult word problem, whether it is ones with variables or numbers, is to approach the problem in simple steps. Do not be intimidated by the length or wording of these often complicated problems. Break the problem down into a series of simpler problems using easy to understand language and then replace that language with variables. Let's take a very difficult variable problem and show how a seemingly overwhelming word problem can be solved successfully using this method.

1.   On a family vacation with his RV, Bill drove a total of x miles. He averaged 50 miles per hour for the entire trip except for a 10 mile section when he averaged only 20 miles per hour because of construction. His travel time for the x mile trip was what percent greater than it would have been if he had been able to travel 50 miles per hour for the entire trip?

(A)   1.5%

(B)   15%

(C) $\frac{50}{x}$%

(D) $\frac{300}{x}$%

(E) $\frac{1500}{x}$%

Step 1: Write out in plain language exactly what you are solving for (or just map out the equation) so that you can insert variables in the next step

In this case we want the percentage increase of the times for two given scenarios: Time for the Actual Trip (T_A) and Time for the Trip at 50MPH (T_{50}). We know from the arithmetic lesson that

$$\text{Percent Change} = \frac{\text{New - Original}}{\text{Original}} \cdot 100\%.$$ This question wants to know how much of a

percent increase it is from Time for Trip at 50MPH to Time for Actual Trip. With this information we can now create an equation that will lead us quickly to the answer:

$$\frac{\text{Time Actual Trip - Time50MPHTrip}}{\text{Time50MPHTrip}} \cdot 100\% = \text{Percent change asked for in problem.}$$

Step 2: Now, simply replace each section in the equation above with the variables and information given in the problem.

Time Actual Trip = Time for 10 Miles During Construction at 20 MPH + Time for Remainder of the Trip at 50 MPH. Because Time $= \frac{\text{distance}}{\text{rate}}$ we know that he spent $\frac{10}{20}$ hrs or $\frac{1}{2}$ hour during construction and $\frac{x-10}{50}$ hrs for the remainder. The total time would then be $\frac{1}{2} + \frac{x-10}{50}$ hrs for the actual trip. Simplify and combine by using a common denominator of 50 and you see that the time for the actual trip $\frac{25}{50} + \frac{x-10}{50} = \frac{x+15}{50}$ hrs. The time for the "make believe" 50MPH trip is much easier as it is again just distance over rate or $\frac{x}{50}$ hrs. Plugging in to our simple language equation from step 1 we see that the answer is

$$\frac{\frac{x+15}{50} - \frac{x}{50}}{\frac{x}{50}} \cdot 100\%$$

Step 3: Almost all of these variable problems require some kind of algebraic manipulation or simplification after you have set it up properly.

Here you must simplify the fractions within fractions by multiplying the top and bottom by 50. After that manipulation you see that $\frac{x+15-x}{x} = \frac{15}{x}$. After multiplying this by 100% the final answer is $\left(\frac{1500}{x}\right)\%$ or E.

> **GMAT Insider:** The most important thing to focus on is what is being asked. Go to the part with the question mark!

Alternative Method: Picking Your Own Numbers

As we discussed in the Data Sufficiency and Problem Solving lessons, one popular method for dealing with these types of questions is to pick values for the variables and then plug them into the answer choices to locate which one is correct. Without question, this is sometimes a faster approach but often it is time-consuming and prone to error. In other words, it will not work all the time and it usually requires understanding the problem just as well as when using variables. Still, it is a legitimate approach for some of these problems so it is worth examining. The previous problem is a good example for this strategy, so let's look at it again.

1.   On a family vacation in his RV, Bill drove a total of x miles. He averaged 50 miles per hour for the entire trip except for a 10 mile section when he averaged only 20 miles an hour because of construction. His travel time for the x mile trip was what percent greater than it would have been if he had been able to travel 50 miles per hour for the entire trip?

(A)   1.5%

(B)   15%

(C) $\frac{50}{x}$%

(D) $\frac{300}{x}$%

(E) $\frac{1500}{x}$%

To use this approach, let's imagine that the trip was 100 miles and x = 100. The time for the actual trip would then be ½ hour for the ten miles and then $\frac{90}{50}$ or 1.8 hours for the remaining 90 miles. The total time for the actual trip if x = 100 miles would be 2.3 hours. The time for the 50MPH trip would be $\frac{100}{50}$ or 2 hrs if x = 100 miles. You must then calculate the percent change just like we did previously, which is $\frac{2.3 - 2}{2} \cdot 100\% = 15\%$ To solve, you must then plug in 100 for x and look for which answer choice gives you 15%. The answer is clearly E.

> *GMAT Insider:* The test makers will create multiple answer choices that will give the same result using certain numbers. If two answer choices appear to be correct using this method then you must try another set of numbers.

Let's look at several more of these difficult word problems to apply these strategies:

2. A certain car company manufactured x cars at a cost of c dollars per car. If a certain number of cars were sold below cost at a sale price of s dollars per car, while the rest of the cars were sold for the normal retail price of n dollars per car, how many cars could the company afford to sell at the sale price in order to break even (no profit and no loss)?

(A) $\dfrac{x(c - n)}{(s - n)}$

(B) $\dfrac{x(n - c)}{(s - n)}$

(C) $\dfrac{x(c - n)}{(s - c)}$

(D) $\dfrac{x(s - n)}{(c - n)}$

(E) $(x - n)(x - s)$

GMAT Insider: One of the ways that word problems are made more difficult on the GMAT is by replacing numbers with variables. Instead of solving for a number, you are asked, for instance, to solve for x in terms of y and z. Students typically do not perform as well on word problems with variables as those with numbers. Why? It is generally easier to get confused with variables and problems with variables often involve more algebra.

3. Both Car A and Car B set out from their original locations at exactly the same time and on exactly the same route. Car A drives from Morse to Houston at an average speed of 65 miles per hour. Car B drives from Houston to Morse at 50 miles per hour and then immediately returns to Houston at the same speed and on the same route. If Car B arrives in Houston 2 hours after Car A, how many hours did it take Car A to make its trip?

(A)   0.50

(B)   1.00

(C)   1.25

(D)   1.33

(E)   2.00

> *How Your Mind Works:* Any time you are given a word problem with lots of information, it is a good idea to organize that information first. Get a sense for what's being asked globally -- what type of question is being asked (ratio, work/rate, conversion, etc.) and what concepts are being tested. Then, convert language into symbols and math using variables that are not confusing (i.e. use "j" for a person named John, or "Dj" for the distance John traveled, etc.).

4. If a phone call costs a cents for the first minute and $\frac{a}{3}$ cents for each additional half-minute, how much would a b minute phone call cost, in cents?

(A) $\dfrac{(2a+2ab)}{27}$

(B) $\dfrac{(a+2ab)}{3}$

(C) $\dfrac{(a+ab)}{300}$

(D) $\dfrac{(a+ab)}{3}$

(E) $\dfrac{ab}{9}$

How Your Mind Works: Though you should always start a word problem by trying to understand the question, if you are totally lost, try turning each sentence into an equation or expression. Sometimes seeing these on paper can spark your understanding and help you solve the question.

Advanced
Word Problems

Quantitative Review

Because the GMAT tests such a large amount of quantitative material, it is extremely helpful to summarize and organize all the different information that can appear on the test. After completing the course, students can use this guide to assess their comfort level in each area and decide where to spend more time in their preparation. Each of these areas is well covered in the Veritas materials and students should use those resources to review areas of weakness.

Arithmetic

Definitions
Arithmetic Number Properties
Factors/Multiples
Calculations
 -Fractions
 -Decimals
Percents
Ratios
Set Theory

Algebra

Exponents/Roots
Algebraic Number Properties
Factoring/Distributing
Algebraic Equations
-Linear
-Quadratic
Inequalities/Absolute Value
Functions
Sequences

Common Word Problems
(Arithmetic and Algebra)

Work/Rate
Distance/Rate
Venn Diagram
Mixture
Weighted Average
Quotient/Remainder
Discount
Profit/Revenue/Cost
Data Interpretation
"In terms of "
Tree Diagram (Organizing Information)
Interest
Measurement

Geometry

Lines/Angles
Triangles
Quadrilaterals
Circles
 Unusual 2-Dimensional Figures
-Pentagons, Hexagons, etc.
3-Dimensional Figures
Coordinate Geometry

Statistics

Mean
Median
Mode
Range
Standard Deviation

Counting Methods

Strict Counting
Combinations
Permutations

Probability

Definitions
Independent vs. Dependent
"At Least" Probability

GMAT Insider: Understand the wrong answers and not just the right ones. There are generally three levels of comprehension of each practice question:
-Why is the right answer correct? Almost all students will seek out this answer, and internalize it for each question.
-Why is the wrong answer incorrect? Most students will consider this whenever they miss a question.
-What about the wrong answer did you like, or why did the wrong answer look right? Fewer students will consider this, but you should. Knowing which devices the test will employ to lower your score is an important way to avoid making mistakes. Seek out these answers, and ask your instructor for assistance in doing so. Instructors have quite a bit of experience with analyzing student mistakes, and can help you find patterns in the errors you make, allowing you to focus on them directly.

To refresh your understanding, let's look at a collection of problems focusing on the Key Concept areas from this list. With each question, the instructor will review some of the important takeaways for the concept being tested.

Review Problems

Percents

5. The population of a small beach town on Australia's east coast grows by
   50% from May 1 to June 1 and then grows by another 50% from June 1 to July 1.
   The population then decreases by 11.11% from July 1 to August 1. By approximately what percentage has the population grown from May 1st to August 1st?

   (A)   50%

   (B)   90%

   (C)   100%

   (D)   200%

   (E)   225%

   Key Review Takeaways: Percent Calculations, Interpreting the Question, "Approximately,"
   Fractions Are Your Friends

Ratios

6.   In a certain department store, the ratio of the number of full-time salespeople to the number of salespeople who are not full-time is 1 to 4. If 5 more full-time salespeople were hired, the ratio would be 2 to 3. How many salespeople are employed by the store?

(A)   5

(B)   9

(C)   13

(D)   15

(E)   18

Key Review Takeaways: Ratio Concepts, Creating Algebraic Equations from Word Problems, Using Answer Choices

Factors

7.   If x and y are nonzero integers and 450x = 120y then which of the following must be an integer?

     I. $\dfrac{xy}{60}$

     II. $\dfrac{15x}{4y}$

     III. $\dfrac{4x}{15y}$

(A)   I Only

(B)   II Only

(C)   I and III

(D)   I and II

(E)   I, II, and III

Key Review Takeaways: Factor Concepts, Prime Factors and Prime Factorization, Lowest Common Multiple, Interpreting the Question

Calculations

8. $\dfrac{(.44444)(.3750)(.4000)}{(.66667)(.16667)(.7500)}$ is closest to

(A)   .6

(B)   .80

(C)   1.20

(D)   1.25

(E)   1.60

Key Review Takeaways: Recognizing Common Fractions, Converting Decimals to Fractions, "Approximately", Fraction Calculations

Exponents and Roots

9.   What is $3^8 + 3^7 - 3^6 - 3^5$?

(A) $(3^5)(2^4)$

(B) $(3^5)(2^6)$

(C) $(3^6)(2^5)$

(D) 6^5

(E)   None of the Above

Key Review Takeaways: Exponent Rules, Algebraic Factoring

Common Algebraic Equations

10.   If $4x^2 + 9y^2 = 100$ and $(2x + 3y)^2 = 150$ then what is the value of $6xy$?

(A) $5(2 + \sqrt{6})$

(B) $10\sqrt{6}$

(C)   25

(D)   50

(E)   100

Key Review Takeaways: Common Algebraic Equations, Algebraic Calculations, Substitution

Inequalities

11.   Is xy > 24?

    (1) y - 2 < x

    (2) 2y > x + 8

(A)   Statement (1) ALONE is sufficient, but statement (2) alone is not sufficient.

(B)   Statement (2) ALONE is sufficient, but statement (1) alone is not sufficient.

(C)   BOTH statements TOGETHER are sufficient, but NEITHER statement ALONE is sufficient.

(D)   EACH statement ALONE is sufficient.

(E)   Statements (1) and (2) TOGETHER are NOT sufficient.

Key Review Takeaways: Rules for Inequalities, Data Sufficiency Techniques

Number Properties

12.   If n and a are positive integers, what is the unit's digit of $n^{4a+2} - n^{8a}$?

     (1) $n = 3$

     (2) a is odd

(A)   Statement (1) ALONE is sufficient, but statement (2) alone is not sufficient.

(B)   Statement (2) ALONE is sufficient, but statement (1) alone is not sufficient.

(C)   BOTH statements TOGETHER are sufficient, but NEITHER statement ALONE is sufficient.

(D)   EACH statement ALONE is sufficient.

(E)   Statements (1) and (2) TOGETHER are NOT sufficient.

Key Review Takeaways: Units Digits Number Properties, Exponents, Odd/Even Number Properties

Geometry

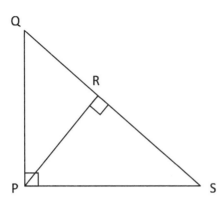

13.   In ΔPQS above, if PQ = 3 and PS = 4, then PR =

(A) $\frac{9}{4}$

(B) $\frac{12}{5}$

(C) $\frac{16}{5}$

(D) $\frac{15}{4}$

(E) $\frac{20}{3}$

Key Review Takeaways: Right Triangles, Area of a Triangle

Interpretation Drill

Do your best to translate each setup into algebraic expressions or equations:

1.   Jack's condo is worth half as much as Jill's house. James' mansion is worth 9 times as much as Jack's condo.

2.   Billy is now three times as old as Jeffrey. In 20 years, Billy will be twice as old as Jeffrey.

3.   An editor predicts that he will find 2 errors per page in a certain document. When he goes through the document, he finds that it actually has 420 total errors, which is 40% higher than his prediction.

4.   The cost to charter a plane is d dollars, which is to be shared equally among the passengers. The number of passengers, which was originally 12, increases to 18, decreasing the cost by x amount per person.

5.   A swimmer swims freestyle at a rate that is twice as fast as his rate on the breaststroke. He swims 2 miles freestyle in a straight line, then swims the breast-stroke back to his starting point in a perfect semicircle. It takes him 20 minutes to swim the freestyle portion.

Facts & Formulas:
(+) is also referred to as: plus, and, added, sum, combined

(-) is also referred to as: minus, less, subtracted, reduced, decreased

(×) is also referred to as: times, product, multiplied, doubled, tripled

(÷) is also referred to as: divided, ratio, over (as in 2 over 3), out of (as in 5 out of 6), per (as in 120 kilometers per hour)

Selected Problems

The next several questions represent topic areas or question types that are particularly difficult for students and warrant special coverage or review. Others are ones that have not been covered in detail in the previous lessons. While you may not have time to cover all of these questions during class, your instructor will select those problems that are best suited for the strengths/weaknesses of your class. For each problem, the question type or topic area will be given.

Sequence

14.   The infinite sequence $a_1, a_2, \ldots, a_n, \ldots$ is such that $a_1 = x$, $a_2 = y$, $a_3 = z$, $a_4 = 3$, and $a_n = a_{n-4}$ for $n > 4$. What is the sum of the first 98 terms of the sequence ?

(1) $x = 5$

(2) $y + z = 2$

(A)   Statement (1) ALONE is sufficient, but statement (2) alone is not sufficient.

(B)   Statement (2) ALONE is sufficient, but statement (1) alone is not sufficient.

(C)   BOTH statements TOGETHER are sufficient, but NEITHER statement ALONE is sufficient.

(D)   EACH statement ALONE is sufficient.

(E)   Statements (1) and (2) TOGETHER are NOT sufficient.

Discount

15. To prepare for the holiday season, a department store increases its prices by fifty percent before marking the prices down by twenty percent. What would be the holiday sale price of an item originally priced at $38.50?

(A) $42.35

(B) $45.80

(C) $46.20

(D) $50.05

(E) $57.75

Statistics

16.   The average (arithmetic mean) of 5 numbers is 6.8. If one of the numbers is multiplied by a factor of 3, the average of the numbers increases to 9.2. What number is multiplied by 3?

(A)   1.5

(B)   3.0

(C)   3.9

(D)   4.0

(E)   6.0

Quotient/Remainder

17. What is the remainder when 33 is divided by the integer y?

(1) $90 < y < 100$

(2) y is a prime number

(A) Statement (1) ALONE is sufficient, but statement (2) alone is not sufficient.

(B) Statement (2) ALONE is sufficient, but statement (1) alone is not sufficient.

(C) BOTH statements TOGETHER are sufficient, but NEITHER statement ALONE is sufficient.

(D) EACH statement ALONE is sufficient.

(E) Statements (1) and (2) TOGETHER are NOT sufficient.

Exponential Increase

18.   The potential energy of a spring is given by the equation, P.E. $= \dfrac{kx^2}{2}$ where k is
a constant and x is the distance the spring is stretched. If k is 16, and the spring
is stretched to 2 feet, then to 3 feet, then how much potential energy is gained
by the spring from the moment it is stretched 2 feet to the moment it is
stretched 3 feet?

(A)   200

(B)   128

(C)   72

(D)   40

(E)   32

Geometry

19.   An equilateral triangle with a side of 6 is perfectly inscribed in a circle. What is the area of the circle?

(A)   3π

(B)   12π

(C)   36π

(D)   48π

(E)   108π

Inverse and Direct Proportions

20.   The variable x is inversely proportional to the square of the variable y. If y is
        divided by 3a, then x is multiplied by which of the following ?

(A) $\dfrac{1}{9a}$

(B) $\dfrac{1}{9a^2}$

(C) $\dfrac{1}{3a}$

(D)   9a

(E) $9a^2$

For the GMAT, it is important to understand both direct and inverse relationships. If two
things are directly proportional then they can be represented algebraically in the
following manner:
x = ky

x is directly proportional to y where k is a constant. In direct proportions, if one variable
gets larger so must the other one.

If one thing is inversely proportional to another, then that relationship can be expressed as
the following:

$xy = k$ or $x = \dfrac{k}{y}$

x is inversely proportional to y where k is a constant. In inverse
proportions, if one variable gets larger than the other must get smaller.

With this knowledge, you can create an equation from the information
given in the problem.

GMAT Insider: Ironically, the best
way to speed up your time on the
GMAT is to slow down. You see, if you
don't carefully read each problem,
you are liable to miss important
principles. And if you don't meticu-
lously pay attention to details as you
solve each problem, you will make
mistakes. Both things will cause you
to either get the problem wrong or
spin your wheels arriving at an answer
that doesn't exist. And that will kill
your time. Or score. Or both.

Last Minute GMAT Tips

1. Don't skim over problems, since you may overlook words. Digest every word!

> "r and s are **not** integers"
> "r, s, t, and u each represent a **nonzero** digit"
> "… can be evenly divided by **neither** 3 nor 5."

2. Be careful to select the answer choice that you meant to select.

3. Speed is the key to a good score on the quantitative section of the GMAT. Work quickly and be focused, but don't rush.

4. If a geometry problem becomes overly complex, there is probably an easier solution. Be careful about your assumptions. Test-takers often make simple mistakes like assuming an angle is 45° when it is 60°. Redraw figures on your laminated noteboard.

5. Heed your inner voice when it tells you "This seems a bit too simple." If it seems too simple, you may be missing something.

6. Write your calculations down on a piece of scrap paper if necessary but try to do simple calculations in your head. Finish problems completely rather than assuming you can see what the answer will be. Remember: Tedious calculations are never required on the GMAT.

7. Be critical of any assumption you make.

> $0.00015 \cdot 10^m = 15 \cdot 10^{(m+5)}$ is not true
> $-2 < -6$ is not true
> x is not necessarily a positive integer

8. When plugging in answer choices, you should usually start with the middle answer choice as the answers are usually ordered in an ascending or a descending order. If your instinct leads you to another choice, or if you believe that another choice would be easier to try, it is okay to start with A, B, C, D, or E.

9. Always use units so that you do not confuse minutes with hours, feet with cubic feet, etc.

10. Memorize probability and counting examples to use as references when you encounter these types of problems on the test. The GMAT is not only a test of the skills you have learned in this course, but also a measure of your mental acuity. You will be sharper when you are properly rested. Sleep a lot the week prior to taking the exam so that you will be rested even if you are nervous the night before the test. Eat safe foods the two days before the test so you don't have any unpleasant distractions. Expect the worst conditions when you take the test: your computer may crash prior to the test, there may be a construction crew working with jack hammers right outside the window, etc. You are prepared for this and nothing can distract you. Enter the test center as focused as an Olympic athlete.

Assorted Problems

21.   A bookstore purchases *x* number of Henry Porter books for sale at *y* dollars per
        book. If overzealous Henry Porter fans steal *s* books and the bookstore
        sells the rest of the books on sale for *z* dollars per book, which of the following
        would represent the gross profit on the sales of the books?

(A) $(x - s)z - xy$

(B) $(x - s)y - sz$

(C) $(z - y)s - xy$

(D) $xy - sz$

(E) $(x - s)(z - y)$

22.   A merchant sells an item at a 20 percent discount, but still makes a gross profit of 20 percent of the cost. What percent of the cost would the gross profit on the item have been if it had been sold without the discount?

(A)   20%

(B)   40%

(C)   50%

(D)   60%

(E)   75%

23.   A milliner bought a lot of hats, $\frac{1}{4}$ of which were brown. The milliner sold $\frac{2}{3}$ of the hats including $\frac{4}{5}$ of the brown hats. What fraction of the unsold hats were brown?

(A) $\frac{1}{60}$

(B) $\frac{2}{15}$

(C) $\frac{3}{20}$

(D) $\frac{3}{5}$

(E) $\frac{3}{4}$

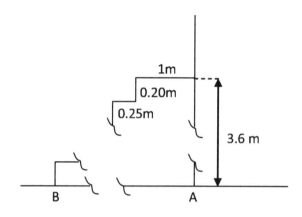

24.   Each step of a staircase is 0.25 meter wide and 0.20 meter high, as shown in the figure above. All angles shown in the figure are right angles. If the height of the staircase is 3.6 meters and the landing at the top of the staircase is 1 meter wide, how long, in meters, is AB?

(A)   3.0

(B)   4.25

(C)   4.5

(D)   5.25

(E)   5.5

25.   How many integers n greater than 10 and less than 100 are there such that, if the digits of n are reversed, the resulting integer is n + 9?

(A)   5

(B)   6

(C)   7

(D)   8

(E)   9

26. A family made a down payment of $75 and borrowed the balance on a set of encyclopedias that cost $400. The balance with interest was paid in 23 monthly payments of $16 each and a final payment of $9. The amount of interest paid was what percent of the amount borrowed?

(A)   6%

(B)   12%

(C)   14%

(D)   16%

(E)   20%

27.   If $x \neq 0$ and $x = \sqrt{4xy - 4y^2}$, then in terms of y, x =

(A)   2y

(B)   y

(C) $\dfrac{y}{2}$

(D) $\dfrac{-4y^2}{1 - 4y}$

(E)   -2y

28.   Solution Y is 30 percent liquid X and 70 percent water. If 2 kilograms of water
       evaporate from 8 kilograms of solution Y and 2 kilograms of solution Y are added
       to the remaining 6 kilograms of liquid, what percent of this new solution is liquid
       X?

(A)   30%

(B) $33\frac{1}{3}$ %

(C) $37\frac{1}{2}$ %

(D)   40%

(E)   50%

29.   What is the remainder when the integer 6r is divided by 3?

(1) r is an integer.

(2) r is not a multiple of 3.

(A)   Statement (1) ALONE is sufficient, but statement (2) alone is not sufficient.

(B)   Statement (2) ALONE is sufficient, but statement (1) alone is not sufficient.

(C)   BOTH statements TOGETHER are sufficient, but NEITHER statement ALONE is sufficient.

(D)   EACH statement ALONE is sufficient.

(E)   Statements (1) and (2) TOGETHER are NOT sufficient.

30. $$\dfrac{1}{\dfrac{1}{0.03} + \dfrac{1}{0.37}} =$$

(A) 0.004

(B) 0.02775

(C) 2.775

(D) 3.6036

(E) 36.036

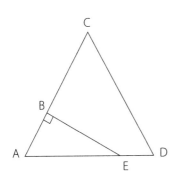

31.   If each side of triangle ACD above has length 3 and if AB has length 1, what is the
       area of region BCDE?

(A) $\dfrac{9}{4}$

(B) $\dfrac{7}{4}\sqrt{3}$

(C) $\dfrac{9}{4}\sqrt{3}$

(D) $\dfrac{7}{2}\sqrt{3}$

(E) $6+\sqrt{3}$

32. $\dfrac{0.025 \cdot \frac{15}{2} \cdot 48}{5 \cdot 0.0024 \cdot \frac{3}{4}} =$

(A) 0.1

(B) 0.2

(C) 100

(D) 200

(E) 1,000

33.   A student responded to all of the 22 questions on a test and received a
       score of 63.5. If the scores were derived by adding 3.5 points for each correct
       answer and deducting 1 point for each incorrect answer, how many questions
       did the student answer <u>incorrectly</u>?

(A)   3

(B)   4

(C)   15

(D)   18

(E)   20

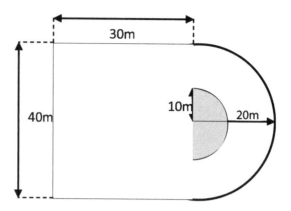

34.   The figure above represents a rectangular parking lot that is 30 meters by 40 meters and an attached semicircular driveway that has an outer radius of 20 meters and an inner radius of 10 meters. If the shaded region is <u>not</u> included, what is the area, in square meters, of the lot and driveway?

(A)   1,350 π

(B)   1,200 + 400 π

(C)   1,200 + 300 π

(D)   1,200 + 200 π

(E)   1,200 + 150 π

35.   One-fifth of the light switches produced by a certain factory are defective. Four-fifths of the defective switches are rejected and $\frac{1}{20}$ of the nondefective switches are rejected by mistake. If all the switches not rejected are sold, what percent of the switches sold by the factory are defective?

(A)   4%

(B)   5%

(C)   6.25%

(D)   11%

(E)   16%

36. In the coordinate geometry plane, a trapezoidal region is enclosed by the following lines: y = 0, y = 4, y = x - 1 and y = -2x + 20 . What is the area of that region?

(A)   8

(B)   12

(C)   24

(D)   26

(E)   30

37.   A group of N families, each with M members are to be lined up in a single line for a photograph. In how many ways can the people be arranged if each family must be kept together?

(A) M^N

(B) $N! \cdot M!$

(C) $N! \cdot M! \cdot N$

(D) $N! \cdot M!^N$

(E) $\dfrac{N!}{(N-M)!}$

38.   If r, s, and t are positive integers and rst = 343, what is the value of t?

(1) r < s < t

(2) rs = 7

(A)   Statement (1) ALONE is sufficient, but statement (2) alone is not sufficient.

(B)   Statement (2) ALONE is sufficient, but statement (1) alone is not sufficient.

(C)   BOTH statements TOGETHER are sufficient, but NEITHER statement ALONE is sufficient.

(D)   EACH statement ALONE is sufficient.

(E)   Statements (1) and (2) TOGETHER are NOT sufficient.

39.   There are 13 South American countries. Arne has won a ticket to fly from Denver, Colorado, to one South American country and then directly to another South American country, before returning home to Denver again. Assuming there are four airports in each country, how many flight paths can Arne choose from?

(A) $13 \cdot 12 \cdot 11 \cdot 10 \cdot 4^2$

(B) $13 \cdot 12 \cdot 11 \cdot 10 \cdot 4$

(C) $13 \cdot 12 \cdot 4^2$

(D) $13 \cdot 12 \cdot 4$

(E) 13^4

40. Earl and four friends go to a ball game. In how many ways can they sit together so that Earl always sits between two friends?

(A)   6

(B)   24

(C)   48

(D)   72

(E)   120

41.   Joe, a truck driver, is paid 45 cents per mile, up to 300 miles per day. For each
      additional mile he drives, he is paid a rate per mile that is 20 cents higher than
      his regular rate. If Joe drives 525 miles on a given day, how much is he paid for
      that day?

(A) $180.00

(B) $203.75

(C) $281.25

(D) $305.50

(E) $326.75

I.   52, 52, 52, 52, 52

II.   36, 52, 52, 52, 71

III.   51, 52, 53, 54, 55

42.   The data sets I, II, and III above are ordered from the least standard deviation to the greatest standard deviation in which of the following?

(A)   I, II, III

(B)   I, III, II

(C)   II, III, I

(D)   II, I, III

(E)   III, II, I

43. Of the CDs at a certain music store, $\frac{1}{6}$ are rock, $\frac{1}{3}$ are pop, $\frac{1}{4}$ are classical, and the remaining 15 CDs are alternative. What is the total number of CDs at the store?

(A) 45

(B) 60

(C) 72

(D) 180

(E) 360

44. The average (arithmetic mean) of 16 students' first quiz scores in a difficult English class is 62.5. If one student decides to drop the class, the average of the remaining scores becomes 64.0. What is the quiz score of the student who dropped?

(A) 10

(B) 25

(C) 40

(D) 55

(E) 70

45.   How many integers x are there such that $0 < 3x + 3 < 48$?

(A)   13

(B)   14

(C)   15

(D)   16

(E)   17

46. Mr. Goldstein, who is interested in purchasing a new vehicle, decides to buy an automobile with a sticker price of $45,500. If the sales tax comes out to 5 percent of the sticker price, but Mr. Goldstein was able to negotiate a 20 percent discount off the sticker price, what would be the amount Mr. Goldstein pays for the sales tax?

(A) $455

(B) $910

(C) $1,560

(D) $1,820

(E) $2,275

47. Set T is a finite set of positive consecutive multiples of 14. How many of these integers are also multiples of 21?

    (1) Set T consists of 30 integers.

    (2) The smallest integer in Set T is a multiple of 21.

(A) Statement (1) ALONE is sufficient, but statement (2) alone is not sufficient.

(B) Statement (2) ALONE is sufficient, but statement (1) alone is not sufficient.

(C) BOTH statements TOGETHER are sufficient, but NEITHER statement ALONE is sufficient.

(D) EACH statement ALONE is sufficient.

(E) Statements (1) and (2) TOGETHER are NOT sufficient.

48. If a birthday cakes weigh 4 pounds each and b wedding cakes weigh 7 pounds each, then the average (arithmetic mean) weight, in pounds per cake, is equal to

(A) $\dfrac{4a + 7b}{a + b}$

(B) $\dfrac{4a + 7b}{ab}$

(C) $\dfrac{4a + 7b}{11}$

(D) $\dfrac{28ab}{a + b}$

(E) $\dfrac{28ab}{11}$

49.   If 5x = 4y, which of the following is NOT true?

(A) $\dfrac{x + y}{y} = \dfrac{9}{5}$

(B) $\dfrac{y}{y - x} = 5$

(C) $\dfrac{x - y}{y} = \dfrac{1}{5}$

(D) $\dfrac{4x}{5y} = \dfrac{16}{25}$

(E) $\dfrac{x + 3y}{x} = \dfrac{19}{4}$

50.   If positive integers a and b are not both even, which of the following must be odd?

(A)   ab

(B)   a + b

(C)   a - b

(D)   a + b - 1

(E)   2(a + b) – 1

51.   The average (arithmetic mean) of 10, 12, and 14 equals the average of 9, 11, and

(A)   12

(B)   13

(C)   14

(D)   15

(E)   16

52.   John is a trail runner who decides to take a day off work to run up and down a local mountain. He runs uphill at an average speed of 5 miles per hour, and returns along the same route at an average speed of 7 miles per hour. Of the following, which is the closest to the average speed, in miles per hour, for the trip up and down the mountain?

(A)   5.5

(B)   5.8

(C)   6.0

(D)   6.3

(E)   6.5

53. Two long-time friends want to meet for lunch on a free weekend. One friend, Ann, lives in Portland, and the other, Bill, lives in Seattle. They decide to meet somewhere along this 200-mile stretch, and start driving simultaneously from their respective cities towards each other along the same route. Ann drives an average of 50 miles per hour, and Bill drives an average of 70 miles per hour. Approximately how many miles from Portland will the two meet?

(A)   56.7

(B)   60.0

(C)   72.5

(D)   83.3

(E)   96.7

54.   If $11m - n = p$, then which of the following represents the average (arithmetic mean) of m, n, and p, in terms of m?

(A)   2m - 1

(B)   4m

(C)   6m

(D) $\dfrac{m}{5}$

(E) $\dfrac{6m}{5}$

55. An epidemic is reported to have broken out in Florida. The number of detected instances of a certain disease is reported to have increased by 85% in the last year. What is the lowest number of newly detected instances possible?

(A)   1

(B)   5

(C)   11

(D)   15

(E)   17

56. Is $\sqrt{7ab}$ an integer?

(1) $a = 7$

(2) b is equal to an integer raised to the third power.

(A)   Statement (1) ALONE is sufficient, but statement (2) alone is not sufficient.

(B)   Statement (2) ALONE is sufficient, but statement (1) alone is not sufficient.

(C)   BOTH statements TOGETHER are sufficient, but NEITHER statement ALONE is sufficient.

(D)   EACH statement ALONE is sufficient.

(E)   Statements (1) and (2) TOGETHER are NOT sufficient.

57.   A bakery sold an average (arithmetic mean) of 820 cookies per day in an operating period. On "good" days, the bakery sold an average of 980 cookies per day, and on "fair" days, the bakery sold an average of 640 cookies per day. What was the ratio of the number of "good" days to the number of "fair" days for the bakery's operating cycle?

(A)   2 : 1

(B)   3 : 2

(C)   5 : 4

(D)   7 : 6

(E)   9 : 8

58.   If a racehorse runs an average (arithmetic mean) of m miles per race for r races, and then runs n miles in its next race, what is the average number of miles the horse has run for the r + 1 races?

(A) $\dfrac{rm + n}{r + 1}$

(B) $\dfrac{m + n}{r + 1}$

(C) $\dfrac{m + n}{r}$

(D) $\dfrac{r(m + n)}{r + 1}$

(E) $\dfrac{m + rn}{r + 1}$

59.   Michael cashed a check for $1,200 and received only $10 and $50 denomina-
        tions in return. During the course of a day, he used 15 bills and then lost the rest
        of the money. If the number of $10 bills used was one more or one less than the
        number of $50 bills used, what is the minimum possible amount of money that
        was lost?

(A) $830

(B) $800

(C) $770

(D) $730

(E) $700

60. On a given week, the classic literature section in a certain library had 40 different books, all of which were in stock on the shelf on Monday morning. If 50 percent of the books that were borrowed during the week were returned to the library on or before Saturday morning of that same week, and if there were at least 22 books on the shelf that Saturday morning, what is the greatest number of books that could have been borrowed during the week?

(A) 40

(B) 38

(C) 36

(D) 34

(E) 32

61. The owner of an art store made profits of $300, $140, $60, and $270 on four separate sales, and has one additional sale pending. If the owner is to receive an average (arithmetic mean) profit of exactly $220 on the five sales, then the fifth commission must be

(A) 370

(B) 330

(C) 270

(D) 230

(E) 150

62. If this year 85 percent of all the sales of an art gallery came from the sale of paintings, and the remaining sales, totaling $330,000, came from the sale of sculptures, what were the total sales for the gallery?

(A) $388,000

(B) $1,300,000

(C) $1,950,000

(D) $2,200,000

(E) $2,550,000

63. Bucket A is $\frac{1}{4}$ full of water and bucket B, which has three times the capacity of bucket A, is $\frac{3}{4}$ full of water. If all the water in bucket A is poured into bucket B, then bucket B will be filled to what fraction of its capacity?

(A)   1

(B) $\frac{1}{2}$

(C) $\frac{5}{6}$

(D) $\frac{11}{12}$

(E) $\frac{7}{6}$

64.   In a certain bacterial population, there are 4 times as many E. Coli bacteria as there are Salmonella bacteria. The ratio of the E. Coli to the total bacterial population is

(A)   1 to 2

(B)   1 to 4

(C)   1 to 5

(D)   3 to 4

(E)   4 to 5

65.   Is *ab* a prime number?

       (1) *a* is a prime number.

       (2) *b* is not a prime number.

(A)   Statement (1) ALONE is sufficient, but statement (2) alone is not sufficient.

(B)   Statement (2) ALONE is sufficient, but statement (1) alone is not sufficient.

(C)   BOTH statements TOGETHER are sufficient, but NEITHER statement ALONE is sufficient.

(D)   EACH statement ALONE is sufficient.

(E)   Statements (1) and (2) TOGETHER are NOT sufficient.

66. A malfunctioning machine at a particular factory increased the number of defects on the production of widgets from 60 to 110 defects per day. By what percent is the number of defects increased by the malfunctioning machine?

(A) $33\frac{1}{3}\%$

(B) 50%

(C) $66\frac{1}{3}\%$

(D) $66\frac{2}{3}\%$

(E) $83\frac{1}{3}\%$

67.   Jonathan is scheduled to take a flight from Boston to Denver, a distance of
       approximately 1950 miles, at an average rate of 650 miles per hour, and should
       arrive in Denver at 2 AM, Denver time. At what hour in Boston time will the plane
       depart for Denver? (Note: Denver time is two hours earlier than Boston time.)

(A)   5 AM

(B)   1 AM

(C)   9 PM

(D)   7 PM

(E)   3 PM

68. A certain used DVD player can be repaired for $36.00 and will last for 2 years of use. A new DVD player of the same make and model can be purchased for $90.00 and will last for 4 years of use. The average cost (per year of use) to purchase the new DVD player is what percent greater than the average cost (per year of use) to repair the used DVD player?

(A)   5%

(B)   10%

(C)   13%

(D)   25%

(E)   50%

69. In the floor of a particular kitchen owned by an abstract artist, each row of tiles directly to the right of the first row contains two fewer tiles than the row next to it. If there are nine rows in all and a total of 504 tiles in the floor, how many tiles does the left-most row contain?

(A)   52

(B)   56

(C)   60

(D)   64

(E)   68

70. A plane traveled k miles in the first 96 minutes of flight time. If it completed the remaining 300 miles of the trip in t minutes, what was its average speed, in miles per hour, for the entire trip?

(A) $\dfrac{60(k + 300)}{96 + t}$

(B) $\dfrac{kt + 96(300)}{96t}$

(C) $\dfrac{k + 300}{60(96 + y)}$

(D) $\dfrac{5k}{8} + \dfrac{60(300)}{t}$

(E) $\dfrac{5k}{8} + 5t$

71. George is in the business of renting out novelty costumes. For each costume he rents out, George receives a commission of $15 plus 20 percent of the rental price. During one particular month, George rented out 50 costumes for prices totaling $7,950. What was the total of George's commissions for that month?

(A) $890

(B) $1,320

(C) $1,680

(D) $1,960

(E) $2,340

72. A lecture course consists of 595 students. The students are to be divided up into discussion sections, each with an equal number of students. Which of the following CANNOT be the number of students in a discussion section?

(A)   17

(B)   35

(C)   45

(D)   85

(E)   119

73. A certain bell at a cathedral marks every hour by ringing a number of times equal to the current hour (for example, at 2:00 p.m., the bell would ring twice). Each toll of the bell lasts for three seconds, with two seconds of silence between each toll. At 9:00 a.m., how many seconds will elapse between the beginning of the first toll and the end of the last toll?

(A)   52

(B)   48

(C)   45

(D)   43

(E)   40

74.
$$\begin{array}{r} 1AB \\ +\ AB \\ \hline CDE \end{array}$$

In the correctly worked sum above, A, B, C, D, and E are single digit integers. What is the value of C?

(1) A < 5

(2) B > 4

(A)   Statement (1) ALONE is sufficient, but statement (2) alone is not sufficient.

(B)   Statement (2) ALONE is sufficient, but statement (1) alone is not sufficient.

(C)   BOTH statements TOGETHER are sufficient, but NEITHER statement ALONE is sufficient.

(D)   EACH statement ALONE is sufficient.

(E)   Statements (1) and (2) TOGETHER are NOT sufficient.

75. Georgia, who lives in a cold area, has 13 pairs of matched gloves in different patterns. If she loses 9 individual gloves, what is the greatest number of pairs of matched gloves she can have left?

(A)   9

(B)   8

(C)   7

(D)   6

(E)   5

76. Jim takes a flight on a plane that flies at 600 miles per hour. If he travels 180 miles, how many minutes does his flight take?

(A)   3

(B) $3\frac{1}{3}$

(C) $8\frac{2}{3}$

(D)   12

(E)   18

77. Last year, for every 100,000 people living in the United States, 390 people suffered from a myocardial infarction. If 350 million people live in the U.S. last year, how many of those people suffered from myocardial infarctions? (1 million = 1,000,000)

(A) 976,000

(B) 1,285,000

(C) 1,365,000

(D) 1,500,000

(E) 1,742,000

78.   What is the least positive integer that is divisible by each of the integers between 3 and 8, non-inclusive?

(A)   420

(B)   840

(C)   1,260

(D)   2,520

(E)   5,040

79.   In a certain accounting association, forty percent of the members have passed
       the CPA exam. Among the members who have not passed the test, 50 members
       work at an accounting firm and the other 55 are still in school. How many
       members are in the accounting association?

(A)   175

(B)   200

(C)   225

(D)   250

(E)   275

80.   How many two-element subsets of {4,5,6,7,8} are there that do not contain the pair of elements 5 and 7?

(A)   Six

(B)   Seven

(C)   Eight

(D)   Nine

(E)   Ten

1,257

1,275

1,527

....

....

+ 7,521

81. The addition problem above shows four of the 24 different integers that can be formed by using each of the digits 1, 2, 5, and 7 exactly once in each integer. What is the sum of these 24 integers?

(A) 26,996

(B) 44,404

(C) 60,444

(D) 66,660

(E) 99,990

82.   What percent of 40 is 16?

(A)   2.5%

(B)   3.6%

(C)   25%

(D)   40%

(E)   250%

83.   What is the average of a, b, and c?

(1) The average of a and b is c.

(2) The average of b and c is 4.

(A)   Statement (1) ALONE is sufficient, but statement (2) alone is not sufficient.

(B)   Statement (2) ALONE is sufficient, but statement (1) alone is not sufficient.

(C)   BOTH statements TOGETHER are sufficient, but NEITHER statement ALONE is sufficient.

(D)   EACH statement ALONE is sufficient.

(E)   Statements (1) and (2) TOGETHER are NOT sufficient.

84.   On a 5-day camping trip, 3 adults consumed freeze-dried meals costing a total of $90. For the same freeze-dried meal costs per person per day, what would be the cost of these meals consumed by 8 adults during a 9-day camping trip?

(A) $450

(B) $432

(C) $374

(D) $346

(E) $288

85.   In a poll of 88,000 dentists, only 30 percent responded; of these, 15 percent
       stated their preference for toothpaste Y. How many of the dentists who
       responded did <u>not</u> state a preference for toothpaste Y?

(A)   16,220

(B)   18,800

(C)   22,440

(D)   26,400

(E)   30,660

86. $\dfrac{2}{100} + \dfrac{4}{1,000} + \dfrac{6}{100,000} =$

(A)   0.246

(B)   0.2406

(C)   0.24006

(D)   0.0246

(E)   0.02406

87.   If the product of the integers a, b, c, and d is 1,155, and if a > b > c > d > 1, what
       is the value of a – d?

(A)   2

(B)   8

(C)   10

(D)   11

(E)   14

88. If vehicle accidents in a certain country occur at the rate of one accident every 45 seconds, how many vehicle accidents on average are there every 2 hours?

(A)   160

(B)   200

(C)   250

(D)   280

(E)   320

89. The value of -10 – (-5) is how much less than the value of -5 – (-10)?

(A)   30

(B)   20

(C)   15

(D)   10

(E)   0

90. Tennis balls are to be placed into 9 buckets so that each bucket contains at least one ball, at the request of detail-oriented players. At most, 5 of the buckets are to contain the same number of balls, and no two of the remaining buckets are to contain an equal number of balls. What is the least possible number of balls needed for the buckets?

(A)   8

(B)   14

(C)   19

(D)   25

(E)   30

	Tax Preparer A	Tax Preparer B
Returns per Day	16	12
Cost per Return	$75	$90

91. The table above gives the cost per tax return to the client and the efficiency with which each of two tax return preparers can complete tax returns in an 8-hour workday. If both preparers decide to work 12 hours on a certain day, how much more gross income can Tax Preparer A make than Tax Preparer B?

(A) $120

(B) $180

(C) $240

(D) $360

(E) $540

92. Liv sold p paintings at an average price of a dollars per painting, and s sculptures at an average price of $550 per sculpture. How much money did Liv receive from the sale of these paintings and sculptures?

(1) s = 3

(2) ap = 2,200

(A) Statement (1) ALONE is sufficient, but statement (2) alone is not sufficient.

(B) Statement (2) ALONE is sufficient, but statement (1) alone is not sufficient.

(C) BOTH statements TOGETHER are sufficient, but NEITHER statement ALONE is sufficient.

(D) EACH statement ALONE is sufficient.

(E) Statements (1) and (2) TOGETHER are NOT sufficient.

93.   A certain electronics store only sells two models of stereos, Stereo X and Stereo Y. The selling price of Stereo X is $540, which is 60 percent of the selling price of Stereo Y. If the electronics store sells 720 stereos, $\frac{2}{3}$ of which are Stereo Y, what is the electronic store's total revenue from the sale of stereos?

(A) $114,400

(B) $186,600

(C) $294,900

(D) $380,800

(E) $561,600

94. At the end of a busy day, a bakery is only left with four packages of 1, 3, 5, and 7 cookies, respectively. Which of the following CANNOT be the total number of cookies of any combination of the packages?

(A)   9

(B)   10

(C)   12

(D)   13

(E)   14

95.   The positive integer x is divisible by 16. If $\sqrt{x}$ is greater than 16, which of the
       following could be the value of $\frac{x}{16}$?

(A)   10

(B)   12

(C)   14

(D)   16

(E)   18

96. Frank earned \$42,000 during the course of a year. He spent $\frac{1}{3}$ of his earnings on rental expenses, and $\frac{2}{5}$ of the remaining amount on food. He found that his utility and miscellaneous expenses together accounted for $\frac{1}{4}$ of his total earnings. If he put whatever amount he had left over into savings, how much money did Frank put into savings?

(A)   \$3,500

(B)   \$4,600

(C)   \$5,000

(D)   \$6,300

(E)   \$7,200

		56
a	b	39
		61

97. In the figure above, the sum of the three numbers in the vertical column equals the product of the three numbers in the horizontal row. What is the value of ab?

(A) 4

(B) 39

(C) 56

(D) 61

(E) 156

98.   For calls made to Madame Leo's psychic hotline, the customer is charged $4.50 per minute during the months of February to June, and $3.00 per minute for calls made during the months of July to January. If the charge for a call placed during May was $36.00, how much would a call of the same duration have cost if it had been placed during December?

(A) $36.00

(B) $24.00

(C) $18.00

(D) $12.00

(E) $9.00

99.   If a hardcover book that usually sells for $24.95 is on sale for $9.95, then the percent decrease in price is closest to

(A)   50%

(B)   53%

(C)   55%

(D)   58%

(E)   60%

100. A banana bread recipe consists of flour, butter, and eggs in the ratio 7 : 4 : 2, respectively, by weight. If 65 pounds of the recipe are prepared, the resulting baked good includes how many more pounds of flour than eggs?

(A) 28

(B) 25

(C) 23

(D) 20

(E) 15

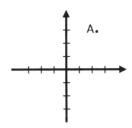

101.   Point A in the figure above has a y-coordinate of 3, and its x-coordinate is nonnegative. What is the x-coordinate of Point A?

(1) The straight-line distance from point A to (0,0) is $\frac{\sqrt{61}}{2}$.

(2) The straight-line distance from point A to the coordinate (3, 0) is $\frac{\sqrt{37}}{2}$.

(A)   Statement (1) ALONE is sufficient, but statement (2) alone is not sufficient.

(B)   Statement (2) ALONE is sufficient, but statement (1) alone is not sufficient.

(C)   BOTH statements TOGETHER are sufficient, but NEITHER statement ALONE is sufficient.

(D)   EACH statement ALONE is sufficient.

(E)   Statements (1) and (2) TOGETHER are NOT sufficient.

102. $(2 + \sqrt{3})(2 - \sqrt{3})$

(A)   -5

(B)   1

(C)   4

(D) $-5 - 4\sqrt{3}$

(E) $4 - 4\sqrt{3}$

103.   The population of a certain species of insects doubles every 20 days. If the
        number of insects in the population was initially 10^3, what was the number in
        the population 300 days later?

(A) $2(10^3)$

(B) $15(10^3)$

(C) $(2^{15})(10^3)$

(D) $(10^{15})(10^3)$

(E) $(10^3)^{15}$

104. If the number of jeans x sold per month at a certain department store varies with the price y in dollars according to the equation x = 1300 – 6y, what would be the total monthly revenue from the sale of a $150 pair of jeans?

(A) $19,500

(B) $54,500

(C) $60,000

(D) $90,000

(E) $105,000

105. Of the 35 flavors of ice cream at an ice cream parlor, 25 flavors contain some sort of nuts, 12 are fat-free, and 8 are both fat-free and contain nuts. How many of the flavors at the ice cream parlor are neither fat-free nor contain nuts?

(A)   6

(B)   10

(C)   14

(D)   20

(E)   25

106. During the fourth quarter of 1999, the revenue for a certain department store was $3,564,000. If this was 32 percent greater than the revenue made during the third quarter of 1999, what was the department store's total revenue during the third quarter?

(A) $752,480

(B) $2,382,540

(C) $2,700,000

(D) $3,470,480

(E) $3,725,000

107.   If a positive integer x is divisible by both 3 and 13, then x must also be divisible
        by which of the following?

        I. 16
        II. 39
        III. 72

(A)   None

(B)   I only

(C)   II only

(D)   I and II

(E)   II and III

108. A music artist is paid $1.20 in royalties for each of the first 50,000 times a song plays on the radio, and $0.80 for each additional airing afterwards. If he is paid a total of $520,000 in royalties, how many times did his song play on the radio?

(A)   150,000

(B)   375,000

(C)   500,000

(D)   625,000

(E)   750,000

109.   Which of the following describes all values of n for which $n^2 - 1 \geq 0$?

(A) $n \geq 1$

(B) $n \leq -1$

(C) $0 \leq n \leq 1$

(D) $n \leq -1$ or $n \geq 1$

(E) $-1 \leq n \leq 1$

110. Two months from now, the population of a colony of insects in a remote area will reach $3.2 \cdot 10^4$. If the population doubles every two months, what was the population eight months ago?

(A) $3.6 \cdot 10^2$

(B) $1.0 \cdot 10^3$

(C) $2.0 \cdot 10^3$

(D) $1.6 \cdot 10^4$

(E) $2.6 \cdot 10^4$

111.   If x = 3y, where y is a prime number greater than 3, how many different positive
        <u>odd</u> divisors does x have, including x?

(A)   One

(B)   Two

(C)   Three

(D)   Four

(E)   Five

112. A is a set containing 7 different numbers. B is a set containing 6 different numbers, all of which are members of A. Which of the following statements CANNOT be true?

(A) The range of A is equal to the range of B.

(B) The mean of A is greater than the mean of B.

(C) The range of A is less than the range of B.

(D) The mean of A is equal to the mean of B.

(E) The median of A is equal to the median of B.

113.   Last year, Bob spent 2 percent of his $75,000 in earnings on entertainment
        expenses. If he placed 60 percent of his total earnings into a high-interest
        savings account, how much money does Bob have left over for other expenses?

(A) $45,000

(B) $43,500

(C) $34,000

(D) $30,000

(E) $28,500

114.   If a and b are integers and $ab - a$ is odd, which of the following must be odd?

(A) b^2

(B) b

(C) $a^2 + b$

(D) ab

(E) $ab + b$

Challenge Problems

115. A seamstress buys 10 buttons and 8 snaps for $23.90. Assuming that all buttons are priced the same, and all snaps are priced the same, what is the price of 1 snap?

    1) If the seamstress had bought the same number of snaps, but only 7 buttons, the total cost would have been $5.25 less.

    (2) If the seamstress had bought 15 buttons and 13 snaps, the total cost would have been $30.00.

(A)   Statement (1) ALONE is sufficient, but statement (2) alone is not sufficient.

(B)   Statement (2) ALONE is sufficient, but statement (1) alone is not sufficient.

(C)   BOTH statements TOGETHER are sufficient, but NEITHER statement ALONE is sufficient.

(D)   EACH statement ALONE is sufficient.

(E)   Statements (1) and (2) TOGETHER are NOT sufficient.

116. Set S consists of the values 11, -9, 100, 0, x, and y, and x ≠ y. What is the median of Set S?

(1) The average (arithmetic mean) of x and y is 308.

(2) The mode of Set S is 0.

(A) Statement (1) ALONE is sufficient, but statement (2) alone is not sufficient.

(B) Statement (2) ALONE is sufficient, but statement (1) alone is not sufficient.

(C) BOTH statements TOGETHER are sufficient, but NEITHER statement ALONE is sufficient.

(D) EACH statement ALONE is sufficient.

(E) Statements (1) and (2) TOGETHER are NOT sufficient.

117.   If $b = 2$, what is the value of a?

(1) $ab = a^2$

(2) $a \neq b$

(A)   Statement (1) ALONE is sufficient, but statement (2) alone is not sufficient.

(B)   Statement (2) ALONE is sufficient, but statement (1) alone is not sufficient.

(C)   BOTH statements TOGETHER are sufficient, but NEITHER statement ALONE is sufficient.

(D)   EACH statement ALONE is sufficient.

(E)   Statements (1) and (2) TOGETHER are NOT sufficient.

118. Is $x > 3$?

(1) The sum of x and the square of x is 12.

(2) $x^2 > 9$

(A)   Statement (1) ALONE is sufficient, but statement (2) alone is not sufficient.

(B)   Statement (2) ALONE is sufficient, but statement (1) alone is not sufficient.

(C)   BOTH statements TOGETHER are sufficient, but NEITHER statement ALONE is sufficient.

(D)   EACH statement ALONE is sufficient.

(E)   Statements (1) and (2) TOGETHER are NOT sufficient.

119.   If x and y are integers, and their sum is 23, is y ≥ 9?

(1) x – 6 < 9

(2) x^3 = 2,744

(A)   Statement (1) ALONE is sufficient, but statement (2) alone is not sufficient.

(B)   Statement (2) ALONE is sufficient, but statement (1) alone is not sufficient.

(C)   BOTH statements TOGETHER are sufficient, but NEITHER statement ALONE is sufficient.

(D)   EACH statement ALONE is sufficient.

(E)   Statements (1) and (2) TOGETHER are NOT sufficient.

120. Over the last three years a scientist had an average (arithmetic mean) yearly income of $45,000. The scientist earned $1\frac{1}{2}$ times as much the second year as the first year and $2\frac{1}{2}$ times as much the third year as the first year. What was the scientist's income the second year?

(A) $9,000

(B) $13,500

(C) $27,000

(D) $40,500

(E) $45,000

121.   How many two-digit whole numbers yield a remainder of 1 when divided by 10
       and also yield a remainder of 1 when divided by 6?

(A)   None

(B)   One

(C)   Two

(D)   Three

(E)   Four

122. If $x \neq 3$ and $\dfrac{x^2 - 9}{2y} = \dfrac{x - 3}{4}$, then in terms of y, x =

(A) $\dfrac{y - 6}{2}$

(B) $\dfrac{y - 3}{2}$

(C) $y - 3$

(D) $y - 6$

(E) $\dfrac{y + 6}{2}$

123.   What is the value of x?

(1) $3x - \frac{1}{4}y = 17$

(2) $-1.5y = 102 - 18x$

(A)   Statement (1) ALONE is sufficient, but statement (2) alone is not sufficient.

(B)   Statement (2) ALONE is sufficient, but statement (1) alone is not sufficient.

(C)   BOTH statements TOGETHER are sufficient, but NEITHER statement ALONE is sufficient.

(D)   EACH statement ALONE is sufficient.

(E)   Statements (1) and (2) TOGETHER are NOT sufficient.

124. Is $\frac{11x}{23} < \frac{7x}{13}$?

(1) x is an integer.

(2) x > 0

(A)   Statement (1) ALONE is sufficient, but statement (2) alone is not sufficient.

(B)   Statement (2) ALONE is sufficient, but statement (1) alone is not sufficient.

(C)   BOTH statements TOGETHER are sufficient, but NEITHER statement ALONE is sufficient.

(D)   EACH statement ALONE is sufficient.

(E)   Statements (1) and (2) TOGETHER are NOT sufficient.

125. What is the least possible product of 4 different integers, each of which has a
      value between -5 and 10, inclusive?

(A)   -5040

(B)   -3600

(C)   -720

(D)   -600

(E)   -120

126.   If a motorist had driven 1 hour longer on a certain day and at an average rate of 5 miles per hour faster, he would have covered 70 more miles than he actually did. How many more miles would he have covered than he actually did had he driven 2 hours longer and at an average rate of 10 miles per hour faster on that day?

(A)   100

(B)   120

(C)   140

(D)   150

(E)   160

127.   If $yz \neq 0$, is $\dfrac{x - y + z}{2z} < \dfrac{x}{2z} - \dfrac{y}{2z} - \dfrac{x}{y}$?

(1) $\dfrac{x}{y} < -\dfrac{1}{2}$

(2) $xy < 0$

(A)   Statement (1) ALONE is sufficient, but statement (2) alone is not sufficient.

(B)   Statement (2) ALONE is sufficient, but statement (1) alone is not sufficient.

(C)   BOTH statements TOGETHER are sufficient, but NEITHER statement ALONE is sufficient.

(D)   EACH statement ALONE is sufficient.

(E)   Statements (1) and (2) TOGETHER are NOT sufficient.

128.   If $x \neq 0$, is $\dfrac{5x-2}{3} - \dfrac{5x-1}{4} > 0$?

(1) $x > 1$

(2) $x = |x|$

(A)   Statement (1) ALONE is sufficient, but statement (2) alone is not sufficient.

(B)   Statement (2) ALONE is sufficient, but statement (1) alone is not sufficient.

(C)   BOTH statements TOGETHER are sufficient, but NEITHER statement ALONE is sufficient.

(D)   EACH statement ALONE is sufficient.

(E)   Statements (1) and (2) TOGETHER are NOT sufficient.

129. Set S consists of consecutively spaced numbers. What is the average (arithmetic mean) of all the numbers in the set?

(1) The nth smallest number in Set S is −7.

(2) The nth largest number in Set S is 13.

(A)   Statement (1) ALONE is sufficient, but statement (2) alone is not sufficient.

(B)   Statement (2) ALONE is sufficient, but statement (1) alone is not sufficient.

(C)   BOTH statements TOGETHER are sufficient, but NEITHER statement ALONE is sufficient.

(D)   EACH statement ALONE is sufficient.

(E)   Statements (1) and (2) TOGETHER are NOT sufficient.

130.   If x, y, and z are distinct prime numbers, how many positive factors does $(xy)^z$ have?

(1) $z = 5$

(2) $x + y = 10$

(A)   Statement (1) ALONE is sufficient, but statement (2) alone is not sufficient.

(B)   Statement (2) ALONE is sufficient, but statement (1) alone is not sufficient.

(C)   BOTH statements TOGETHER are sufficient, but NEITHER statement ALONE is sufficient.

(D)   EACH statement ALONE is sufficient.

(E)   Statements (1) and (2) TOGETHER are NOT sufficient.

131.   If an organization were to sell *n* tickets for a theater production, the total revenue from ticket sales would be 20 percent greater than the total costs of the production. If the organization actually sold all but 5 percent of the *n* tickets, the total revenue from ticket sales was what percent greater than the total costs of the production?

(A)   4%

(B)   10%

(C)   14%

(D)   15%

(E)   18%

132. When the integer n is divided by 6, the remainder is 3. Which of the following is NOT a multiple of 6?

(A) $n - 3$

(B) $n + 3$

(C) $2n$

(D) $3n$

(E) $4n$

133.   How many liters of pure alcohol must be added to a 100-liter solution that is 20 percent alcohol in order to produce a solution that is 25 percent alcohol?

(A) $\dfrac{7}{2}$

(B)   5

(C) $\dfrac{20}{3}$

(D)   8

(E) $\dfrac{39}{4}$

134. If 10 persons meet at a reunion and each person shakes hands exactly once with each of the others, what is the total number of handshakes?

(A) $10 \cdot 9 \cdot 8 \cdot 7 \cdot 6 \cdot 5 \cdot 4 \cdot 3 \cdot 2 \cdot 1$

(B) $10 \cdot 10$

(C) $10 \cdot 9$

(D) 45

(E) 36

Solutions

Interpretation Drill Solutions

There is often more than one way to translate a problem setup into algebra. The following answers do not represent the only ways to translate these problems – however, they do represent approaches that are direct and often simpler than alternate methods.

1. Since all the names begin with "J", represent the homes' values with different letters. Let c = Jack's condo's value, h = Jill's house's value, and m = James's mansion's value. Then:

$$c = \frac{h}{2}$$
$$m = 9c$$

2. The most common mistake in problems of this kind is forgetting to add 20 years to Jeffrey as well as to Billy in the second equation:

$$b = 3j$$
$$b + 20 = 2(j+20)$$

3. Since the number of errors changes from predicted to actual, you must make this distinction in your notation. Sometimes you will need two different variables. Here, the number of actual errors is given to you, so this isn't strictly necessary, but it is still good to be explicit in your scratchwork to avoid confusion. You may want to write down what your variables represent:

errors (predicted) = e

pages = p

$$\frac{e}{p} = 2$$

$$420 = e + .4e \rightarrow 420 = 1.4e$$

4. Sometimes, if you won't be manipulating a quantity, it may be easier to simply define it in terms of other variables without giving it a variable itself. In this question, you can define "original cost per person" and "new cost per person" in this way:

total cost = d

$$\frac{\text{orig. cost}}{\text{person}} = \frac{d}{12}$$

new cost per person = $\frac{d}{18}$

$$x = \frac{d}{12} - \frac{d}{18} \rightarrow x = \frac{d}{36}$$

5. In this rate problem, even though the same person is swimming both freestyle and breaststroke, nothing is equivalent – not the rate, the distance, or the time. In this situation, you should use subscripts to distinguish between freestyle and breaststroke while working with the $d = rt$ equation. It is also a good idea to draw a diagram so that you are clear on the geometry of this setup :

$r_f = 2r_b$

$d_f = 2$

$d_b = \pi$. [The semicircle's length is half the circumference: $\frac{\pi \cdot \text{diameter}}{2}$, or π.]

$t_f = 20$

$d = rt$, therefore $2 = r_f(20)$ and $\pi = r_b t_b$

Lesson Solutions

1. **(E)**

In this case we want the percentage increase of the times for two given scenarios: Time for the Actual Trip (T_A) and Time for the Trip at 50MPH (T_{50}) We know from the arithmetic lesson that

$\text{Percent Change} = \dfrac{\text{New - Original}}{\text{Original}} \cdot 100\%$. This question wants to know how much of a percent

increase it is from Time for Trip at 50MPH to Time for Actual Trip. With this information we can now create an equation that will lead us quickly to the answer:

$\dfrac{\text{Time Actual Trip- Time50MPHTrip}}{\text{Time50MPHTrip}} \cdot 100\% = \text{Percent change asked for in problem.}$

Time Actual Trip = Time for 10 Miles During Construction at 20 MPH + Time for Remainder of the Trip at 50 MPH. Because $\text{Time} = \dfrac{\text{distance}}{\text{rate}}$ we know that he spent $\dfrac{10}{20}$ hrs or $\dfrac{1}{2}$ hour during construction and

$\dfrac{x - 10}{50}$ hrs for the remainder. The total time would then be $\dfrac{1}{2} + \dfrac{x - 10}{50}$ hrs for the actual trip. Simplify and combine by using a common denominator of 50 and you see that the time for the actual trip is

$\dfrac{25}{50} + \dfrac{x - 10}{50} = \dfrac{x + 15}{50}$ hrs. The time for the "make believe" 50MPH trip is much easier as it is again just distance over rate or $\dfrac{x}{50}$ hrs. Plugging this into our simple language equation

from step 1, we see that the answer is $\dfrac{\frac{x + 15}{50} - \frac{x}{50}}{\frac{x}{50}} \cdot 100\%$

Here you must simplify the fractions within fractions by multiplying the top and bottom by 50. After that manipulation you see that $\dfrac{x + 15 - x}{x} = \dfrac{15}{x}$. After multiplying this by 100% the final answer is $\left(\dfrac{1500}{x}\right)\%$ or E.

2. **(A)**

As you learned in the previous example, the first step is to create an equation using plain language and then replace with variables. As this is a Profit = Revenue – Costs problem you know that at the break even point, profit = 0 and Costs = Revenue.

Starting Equation: Costs = Revenue

Because there are two types of revenue – revenue from normal cars and revenue from sale cars – let's make the equation more detailed.

Costs = Revenue from Sale Cars + Revenue from Normal Cars

Also, revenue = (price)(number of items sold) and costs = (cost per item) (the number of items) so let's insert those as well:

(# of cars)(cost per car) = (# of sale cars)(price sale car) +(# of normal cars)(price normal car)

Now, you must insert the variables given in the problem. Also, on this problem you must create and insert a variable for what we are solving for. Let's call the number of sale cars sold at breakeven y.

(# of cars)(cost per car) = (# of sale cars)(price sale cars) + (#of normal cars)(price normal cars)

$$xc = (y)(s) + (x - y)(n)$$

The key to this problem is to realize that the number of normal cars can be expressed as the total cars (x) – sale cars (y). Many people create another variable for normal cars but then it is impossible to solve for y in terms of x, c, and n. The final step on this problem is to isolate the variable y as that is what the problem is asking for. To do that, first remove all parentheses: $xc = ys + xn - yn$

Isolate y on one side of the equation: $xc - xn = ys - yn$

Factor out x and y: $x (c - n) = y (s - n)$

Divide both sides by $(s - n)$: $y = \dfrac{x(c - n)}{(s - n)}$ The answer is A.

3. (C)

Any time you are given a word problem with lots of information, it is a good idea to organize that information first. Here is a summary of all the information, written as equations, that is given in this problem:

1. Rate A (R_a) = 65

2. Rate B (R_b) = 50

3. Distance B (D_b) = 2 (Distance A(D_a)) "Round Trip"

4. Time B (T_b) = Time A (T_a) + 2 "B arrived 2 hours after A"

Let's start with the 2 simple equations that we know are true (D=RT) and then start substituting the information:

$D_a = R_a T_a$ and $D_b = R_b T_b$

From the 3rd piece of information above you know that $D_b = 2(D_a)$ and you can substitute from the two equations above and show that $R_b T_b = 2(R_a T_a)$

The rates are given, so you can plug those in and see that $50T_b = 2(65T_a)$ or $50T_b = 130T_a$

One more substitution for time from the 4th piece of information ($T_b = T_a + 2$) and it is clear that $50 (T_a + 2) = 130T_a$ and $50T_a + 100 = 130T_a$ or $80T_a = 100$. Therefore $T_a = \frac{100}{80}$ or $\frac{5}{4}$.

Therefore the correct answer is C (1.25).

4. (B)

The total number of half-minutes in the phone call is $2b$. The charge for the first 2 half-minutes is a, and the charge for the remaining ($2b$ - 2) half-minutes is ($2b$ - 2) $\cdot \frac{a}{3}$. The total charge of the call is $a + \left(\frac{(2ba-2a)}{3}\right) = \frac{(3a+2ba-2a)}{3} = \frac{(a+2ab)}{3}$. Thus, the answer is B.

5. (C)

With percent questions, it is particularly important to read the question carefully so that you do not misinterpret it. On this question, you must also note the word "approximately" – an important trigger word on any GMAT problem. To solve this quickly, you can either use a variable or pick a number for the starting population (100 is used in the following calculations) Because of the word "approximately," you should recognize that 11.11% is an approximation of a common fraction ($\frac{1}{9}$th) and complete these calculations in fractions. If you work in decimals, the calculations are very tedious.

(Remember: Fractions are your friends.)

May 1st 50% Increase June 1st 50% Increase July 1st 11.11% Decrease Aug. 1st

$$100 \cdot \frac{3}{2} \qquad 150 \cdot \frac{3}{2} \qquad 225 \cdot \frac{8}{9} \quad = 200$$

Note: It is not necessary to calculate the intermediate amounts. The best method is to simply calculate

$100 \cdot \frac{3}{2} \cdot \frac{3}{2} \cdot \frac{8}{9}$ by cancelling the fractions as you go. As the question asks for the percent increase over that time period, you should take the difference between the new value and the old value

(200 – 100 =100) and compare to the original (100).

$\frac{100}{100} \cdot 100\% = 100\%$ Answer is C.

6. **(D)**

Let f be the number of full-time salespeople and p be the number of salespeople who do not work full-time at the department store. Thus, the ratio of $\frac{f}{p} = \frac{1}{4}$. If the number of full-time salespeople increased by 5, the ratio of $\frac{f+5}{p} = \frac{2}{3}$. From the first equation, $f = \frac{1}{4}p$, and from the second equation, $f + 5 = \frac{2}{3}p$,

or $f = \frac{2}{3}p - 5$. Thus, $\frac{2}{3}p - 5 = \frac{1}{4}p$ or $\frac{2}{3}p - \frac{1}{4}p = 5 \rightarrow \frac{5}{12}p = 5$

Therefore, $p = 12$ and $f = \frac{1}{4}(12) = 3$, and the total number of salespeople is

$f + p = 12 + 3 = 15$.

Thus, the answer is (D).

7. **(D)**

If x and y must be integers and $450x = 120y$ then we know certain things about the factors that x and y must contain. After determining those factors, we can assess each of the three statements fairly quickly. A good way to approach this problem is to think of it as a lowest common multiple problem. In other words, let's find the first number on the number line that both 450 and 120 divide into (the lowest common multiple) and see what we learn about x and y. This can be achieved in two ways: 1. Use the numbers given and do the prime factorization of each number and use that information to find the lowest common multiple (LCM). 2. Simplify the equation first and remove all common factors that exist in

the two numbers and then find the LCM (faster). Using the 2nd method, if you divide each side of the equation by 30, then it is simplified to $15x = 4y$. The lowest common multiple of 15 and 4 is 60, so it is clear that x must contain a 4 (2 · 2) and y must contain 15 (3 · 5) to make this equation true. If x and y contain any other numbers in addition to those, they must be the same in each variable or the equation would not be true. In other words, x could also contain a 10 and be 40 (4 · 10) but then y must also contain a 10 and be 150 (15 · 10). To finish the question you have to take these qualities of x and y and decide which one of the statements must be an integer. Looking at I, it is clear that this expression will always be an integer because x and y will always contain 4 · 15, which is 60, guaranteeing an integer. In statement II, the top will contain 15 · 4 and the bottom will contain 4 · 15 which will cancel out leaving an integer. In statement III the factors are reversed and you cannot be sure that it will be an integer:

$\frac{4 \cdot 4}{15 \cdot 15}$ is not an integer so statement III does not guarantee an integer. Note: to solve this effectively just replace x with 4 and y with 15 and see what creates an integer.

8. **(B)**

One way to approach this question is to recognize that the decimals in the expression are approximations of fractions. For example, 0.44444 is approximately $\frac{4}{9}$ and .16667, which is half of .33333, is approximately $\frac{1}{6}$. The expression is approximately $\frac{\left(\frac{4}{9}\right)\left(\frac{3}{8}\right)\left(\frac{2}{5}\right)}{\left(\left(\frac{2}{3}\right)\left(\frac{1}{6}\right)\left(\frac{3}{4}\right)\right)}$. This fractional expression can be written as $\left(\frac{4}{9}\right)\left(\frac{3}{8}\right)\left(\frac{2}{5}\right)\left(\frac{3}{2}\right)\left(\frac{6}{1}\right)\left(\frac{4}{3}\right) = \frac{4}{5} = 0.80$. Thus, 0.80 best approximates this expression, and the answer is B.

9. **(D)**

As with many algebra problems on the GMAT, this example requires students to simplify the given expression and prove which one of the answer choices is equivalent. To simplify $3^8 + 3^7 - 3^6 - 3^5$ it is necessary first to factor out what is in common with each term. In this case that is 3^5 and after factoring you have $3^5(3^3 + 3^2 - 3 - 1)$. It is then possible to simplify the terms within the parentheses as follows: $3^5(27 + 9 - 3 - 1)$ which is $3^5(32)$. Looking at the answer choices, it is clear that you should simplify further as 32 is really 2^5. After that step, you are left with $(3^5)(2^5)$. Unfortunately, this is not an answer choice, so you should look to manipulate further. Remember from your exponent rules that $(x \cdot y)^a = x^a \cdot y^a$ so $(3 \cdot 2)^5 = 3^5 \cdot 2^5$. In other words, $(3^5)(2^5)$ is the same as 6^5 and the answer is D.

10. **(C)**

As you learned in the Algebra book, there are many problems on the GMAT that require you to work with the common algebraic equations:

$(x + y)^2 = x^2 + 2xy + y^2$

$(x - y)^2 = x^2 - 2xy + y^2$

$x^2 - y^2 = (x + y)(x - y)$

Remember that those equations are templates that you can apply to any algebraic equation that is in one of those forms. In this problem you must first expand $(2x + 3y)^2$ using the template above to see that it equals $4x^2 + 12xy + 9y^2$, or written another way $(4x^2 + 9y^2) + 12xy = 150$. In the first equation we are told that $4x^2 + 9y^2 = 100$ so it is possible to substitute that value into the second equation to see that $(100) + 12xy = 150$. Therefore $12xy = 50$ and $6xy = 25$. Answer is C.

11. **(C)**

Inequality questions in Data Sufficiency form are one of the most difficult question types on the GMAT. The common mistake that most students make is to pick numbers to reason out a solution rather than apply conceptual understanding and algebraic manipulation. Number picking has its place on these problems (some can only be solved using numbers to show patterns, etc.) but most can be solved quickly and efficiently with algebra. In this example, it should be fairly clear that each statement is insufficient by itself. In statement 1, we are given a relationship between x and y but we have no idea where those num-

bers are on the number line. For instance, x and y could 0 and 1 or they could be 1000 and 2000. Clearly we know nothing about the size of their product (xy) and so we can't answer the question. The same holds true for the second statement. However, the choice between C and E is fairly difficult and students must use algebra to get a definitive answer. Using your understanding of combining inequalities, it is possible to isolate x and y and learn more about them individually. First let's eliminate x and isolate y:

Step 1: Rewrite the inequalities to line up variables

$y - x < 2$

$2y - x > 8$

Step 2: Multiply top inequality by -1 to get the signs pointing the same way and then combine to

eliminate x:

$-y + x > -2$

$\underline{2y - x > 8}$

$y > 6$

Repeat step 2 to eliminate y by multiplying the top inequality by -2 to get the signs pointing the same way and then combine:

$-2y + 2x > -4$

$\underline{\ 2y - x > 8\ }$

$x > 4$

If $y > 6$ and $x > 4$ then you know that the product of xy must be greater than 24 and the answer to the question is C. Attempting to do this with number picking is both time consuming and ineffective .

12. **(A)**

In the Algebra Lesson packet, you learned that all numbers have a repeating pattern of units digits when they are raised to certain powers. For instance here is the progression for 3:

Units Digit of $3^1 = 3$

Units Digit of $3^2 = 9$

Units Digit of $3^3 = 7$

Units Digit of $3^4 = 1$

Units Digit of $3^5 = 3$

Units Digit of $3^6 = 9$

Units Digit of $3^7 = 7$

Units Digit of $3^8 = 1$

As you can see, the pattern repeats every 4 and it is possible to determine the units digit of any number ending in 3 raised to any power. This data sufficiency question is asking if you can determine the units digit of $n^{4a+2} - n^{8a}$. In other words, if you can determine the units digit of each of those terms then it will be possible to calculate the difference between their units digits. In statement (1) you learn that n is 3 and it seems like you must also know something about a to answer the question. However, a closer look at the exponents shows that it does not matter what value a is. Remember that 3 raised to any multiple of 4 will always end in 1 (for instance 3^{12} or 3^{24}), and 3 raised to any multiple of 4 + 2 (for instance 3^{16} or 3^{26}) will always end in 9. Therefore regardless of what a is, n^{4a+2} will end in 9 and n^{8a} will end in 1. Therefore we can answer the question and the answer must be A or D. A quick look at statement (2) makes it clear that we must know something about n to answer the question and the answer is A.

13. **(B)**

Reference the Veritas Geometry book for help with triangles.

First, either by Pythagorean Theorem or knowledge of special triangles like the 3-4-5 or 5-12-13 triangles, it can be determined that QS is 5.

One way to calculate PR is to use Pythagorean Theorem to express different sides in terms of PR, but this method results in a radical equation that is tedious to solve.

A quicker way to find PR is to note that it is the altitude from P to side QS. Since the area of

a triangle is equal to $\frac{1}{2}$ the product of the length of any side and the length of the altitude to that side, the area can be calculated in two different ways: $= \frac{1}{2}(5)\,(\overline{PR}) = \frac{1}{2}(3 \cdot 4) \rightarrow \overline{PR} = \frac{12}{5}$

Therefore, the answer is B.

14. **(E)**

In any sequence problem, it is first necessary to understand the sequence and then write out some terms to clarify it. Here you are told that $a_n = a_{n-4}$ for $n > 4$ so the first few terms in the sequence are:

$a_1 = x$ $a_5 = a_{5-4} = a_1 = x$ and so on…..

$a_2 = y$ $a_6 = a_{6-4} = a_2 = y$

$a_3 = z$ $a_7 = a_{7-4} = a_3 = z$

$a_4 = 3$ $a_8 = a_{8-4} = a_4 = 3$

What you see is that this formula defines a sequence that repeats every 4 terms to infinity. The goal of the data sufficiency question is to determine the sum of the first 98 terms given this sequence. From Statement (1) we learn x, but nothing about the values of y and z, so we could never determine the sum of the first 98 terms.

Like statement (1), statement (2) does not give us the values of the all of the unknowns so we could never determine their sum.

The difficult choice is between C and E. With the two statements together, we know that the sum of the 4 terms in the sequence is $5 + 2 + 3$, which is 10. If the question asked us about the sum of the first 80 terms, for instance, we would know that every 4 terms adds to 10 and there would be 20 sets of those 4 terms in 80. The sum would thus be 200. However, this question is asking for the first 98 terms. If you divide 98 by 4 you see that there are 24 sets of 4 in 98 with a remainder of 2. In other words, the sum of the first 98 terms is 24 (10) + the next two terms, which are $x + y$. Because there is no way to determine the value of y (we only know the sum of y and z) we cannot determine the sum of the first 98 terms and the answer is (E).

15. **(C)**

An item originally priced at $38.50 is increased by 50%, then decreased by 20%. This can be expressed mathematically as $\$38.50 \cdot 1.5 \cdot 0.8 = \$38.50 \cdot 1.2 = \$46.20$. Thus, the answer is C. To solve $\$38.50 \cdot 1.2$ in your head, think of 1.2 as $1\frac{1}{5}$. So, you can add $\$38.50 + \left(\frac{\$38.50}{5}\right) = \$38.50 + \left(\frac{\$35}{5}\right) + \left(\frac{\$3.50}{5}\right) = \$38.50 + \$7.00 + \$0.70 = \$46.20$.

16. **(E)**

This problem is difficult. First, if the average of 5 numbers is 6.8, it is understood that the sum of those 5 numbers is $6.8 \cdot 5 = 34$. Multiplying one number by a factor of 3 results in the average jumping to 9.2, or the sum of the numbers increasing to $9.2 \cdot 5 = 46$.

Thus, two equations can be formed: $x + y = 34$ and $3x + y = 46$, where x represents the number multiplied by 3, and y represents the sum of the remaining numbers (they do not change). Substitution or addition can be used to solve the series of equations.

Using the addition method, the equations should be lined up, and one should be multiplied by -1 to cancel out the y-variable:

$$3x + y = 46 \rightarrow \quad 3x + y = 46$$
$$x + y = 34 \ (-1) \rightarrow \quad \underline{-x - y = -34}$$
$$2x = 12 \rightarrow x = 6$$

Alternatively, since the difference between the two sums is $46 - 34 = 12$, it can be deduced that multiplying one number by a factor of 3 increases the sum by 12. Where n represents any number, the following equation applies:

Before: $x = n$

After: $3x = n + 12$

Through addition/substitution, it can be calculated that the change of $2x$ on the left of the equation results in a change of 12 on the right. Substituting the first equation into the second shows:

$$3(n) = n + 12 \rightarrow 2n = 12 \rightarrow n = 6 = x$$

Thus, answer choice E is the correct response.

The area of the trapezoid is then $\left(\frac{9+3}{2}\right)(4) = 24$

Answer is C.

17. **(A)**

Conceptually, Quotient/Remainder problems are some of the most difficult on the GMAT. This tricky Data Sufficiency problem is testing one property of remainders that is important to remember: whenever you divide a smaller integer by a larger integer, the remainder is always the dividend (the smaller integer).

Consider this example to see why: 15 goes into 10 zero times leaving a remainder of 10.

$$15\overline{)10}$$
with quotient 0 above and 0 below.

R = 10

From Statement 1, even though we do not the exact value of y, we know that if we divide 33 by any of the possible values for y (91 to 99, inclusive), the remainder is going to be 33. Therefore statement (1) is sufficient to determine the value of the remainder and the answer is A or D. Looking at statement 2, it is clearly insufficient as y could be any prime number, yielding many different remainders when dividing into 33. Clearly, the test makers want you to pick C here as taking the two together allows you to determine that y is 97 and you would be sure of the remainder. The trick is to realize that you don't need statement 2 to solve this problem.

18. **(D)**

When stretched by 2 feet the spring has $\frac{1}{2}(16)(2)^2 = 32$ units of potential energy. When stretched by 3 feet the spring has $\frac{1}{2}(16)(3)^2 = 72$ units of potential energy. This means the spring gained 40 units of potential energy over that distance. The correct answer is D.

19. **(B)**

To find the area of a circle, you need to use the circle area formula, $A = \pi r^2$, which means that you need to find the radius. Draw two radii from the center of the circle (call it C) to two vertices of the equilateral triangle (call them A and B) as shown. This will form an isosceles triangle ABC. The two radii cut the two angles of the equilateral triangle exactly in half. Since equilateral triangles have all 60-degree angles, the small angles of the isosceles triangle must be 30 degrees. If you draw a perpendicular from C to the base of the isosceles triangle (call this point D), you will form right triangle BCD. Since you know two of the angles are 30 degrees and 90 degrees, triangle BCD is a 30-60-90 triangle. The sides of a 30-60-90 triangle correspond to the ratio $1:\sqrt{3}:2$. Set up a proportion to solve for the radius BC:

$$\frac{BD}{BC} = \frac{\sqrt{3}}{2}$$

Side BD is half of AB, so it has a length of 3:

$$\frac{3}{BC} = \frac{\sqrt{3}}{2}$$

Solve for BC:

$$\frac{3}{BC} = \frac{\sqrt{3}}{2} \rightarrow BC = \frac{6}{\sqrt{3}}$$

Plug this into the circle area formula:

$$A = \pi \left(\frac{6}{\sqrt{3}}\right)^2 = \left(\frac{36}{3}\right)\pi = 12\pi$$

The answer is B.

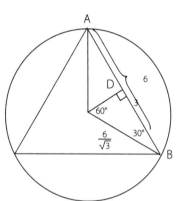

20. **(E)**

You are told that x is inversely proportional to the square of y so $x = \frac{k}{y^2}$. If y is divided by $3a$ then we know that x must be multiplied by the square of $3a$ to offset that change: $(3a)^2 = 9a^2$. In an equation you see that $x = \frac{k}{\left(\frac{y}{3a}\right)^2}$ or $\frac{k}{\frac{y^2}{9a^2}}$. Multiplying top and bottom by $9a^2$, you see that x would now equal $9a^2\left(\frac{k}{y^2}\right)$ if y is divided by $3a$, so the answer is E.

Assorted Solutions

21. **(A)**

Note that Profit = Income − Cost.

The bookstore paid xy dollars for the books, so xy is the cost of the books. The bookstore then sold $(x − s)$ books for z dollars per book, so the total income was $(x − s)z$ dollars. The gross profit, or income minus cost, was therefore $(x − s)z − xy$. Thus, the answer is a).

Alternatively, plug in numbers to obtain the answer to the problem. If the bookstore purchases $x = 10$ books at $y = \$2$ per book, $s = 5$ books were stolen, and the rest of the books were sold at $z = \$7$ per book, then the cost of the books was $20 (10 \cdot \$2)$, and the income was $35 ([10 − 5] \cdot \$7)$. Thus, the profit is $15 (\$35 - \$20)$. Only answer A fits .

22. **(C)**

Let x represent the price before the 20 percent discount and let c represent the cost. Then the merchant sold the item for $0.8x$, which was equal to 120% of the cost c.

Algebraically, the relationship is:

$0.8x = 1.2c$ and $x = 1.5c =$ cost plus 50% profit.

Thus, had the item been sold at the original price, the gross profit would have been 50 percent of the cost. Therefore, the answer is C.

23. **(C)**

Let t be the total number of hats in the lot. Then, from the information in the problem, the following table of values can be assembled:

Hats sold: $\frac{2t}{3}$ Brown hats: $\frac{1}{4}t$

Hats unsold: $\frac{t - 2t}{3} = \frac{t}{3}$ Brown hats sold: $\frac{4}{5}\left(\frac{t}{4}\right) = \frac{t}{5}$

                            Brown hats unsold: $\frac{1}{5}\left(\frac{t}{4}\right) = \frac{t}{20}$

To find the fraction of the unsold hats that were brown, it is necessary to take the ratio of brown hats unsold $\left(\frac{t}{20}\right)$ to total unsold hats $\left(\frac{t}{3}\right)$.

The ratio $\frac{t}{20} : \frac{t}{3} = \dfrac{\frac{t}{20}}{\frac{t}{3}} = \frac{3}{20}$. Thus, the answer is C.

24. (D)

The sum of the widths of the steps, including the landing, is equal to the length of AB. This can be seen by projecting the width of each step onto segment AB. Therefore, to find the length of AB, it is sufficient to find the number of steps, each 0.25 meters wide, and then to add on the 1-meter width of the landing at the top. Since the rise (total height) up to the last step before the landing is 3.6 - 0.20 or 3.4 meters, you can find the number of steps by dividing this total height by the height of each step. Thus, $3.4 \div 0.20 = 17$ steps, and length AB is $17(0.25) + 1 = 5.25$ meters.

Thus, the answer is D.

25. (D)

To solve a problem that involves the digits of a number, it is convenient to let t represent the tens digit and u represent the units' digit.

Since n is between 10 and 100, n is a two-digit number that has the value $10t + u$, and $n + 9$ can be represented by the expression $(10t + u) + 9$. If the digits of n are reversed, the value of the resulting integer will be $10u + t$. According to the problem, $10u + t = n + 9$ or $10u + t = (10t + u) + 9$, which simplifies to $u = t + 1$. In other words, n must be a two-digit number in which the units digit is one more than the tens digit. The eight numbers that have this property are 12, 23, 34, 45, 56, 67, 78, and 89.

Thus, the answer is D.

26. (D)

This problem needs to be broken into two parts.

The family had to borrow $400 - $75 = $325.

They paid back 23(16) + $9 = $377.

The interest they paid can be found in the difference between these two numbers.

They paid $377 - $325 = $52 in interest, which was $\frac{52}{325}$ = 16% of the amount borrowed.

Thus, the answer is D.

27. **(A)**

The value of x can be expressed in terms of y with the following steps:

$x = \sqrt{(4xy - 4y^2)}$ (square both sides)

$x^2 = 4xy - 4y^2$ (make all factors equal to 0)

$x^2 - 4xy + 4y^2 = 0$ (factor)

$(x - 2y)^2 = 0$ (take the square root of both sides)

$(x - 2y) = 0$ (add 2y to both sides)

Therefore, answer choice A is the correct response.

28. **(C)**

The original 8 kilograms (kg) of solution y contains 30% of liquid x, or 2.4 kg liquid x. If 2 kg of water evaporate from the 8 kg, that would leave 6kg, of which 2.4 kg is liquid x. If 2 kg of solution y is added to the remaining 6 kg of solution, the resulting 8 kg-solution would contain 2.4 + 0.3(2) kg of liquid x, which is 2.4 + 0.6 = 3.0 kg

Therefore, the percent of liquid x in the new solution would be: $2.4 + \frac{0.6}{8.0} = \frac{3.0}{8.0} = 37\frac{1}{2}\%$

Thus, the answer is C.

29. **(A)**

Remainders are integer values that are "left over" after performing division. For example, 11 divided by 5 has a remainder of 1, since 5 goes into 11 twice with 1 "left over."

Since 6 is divisible by 3, 6r will be evenly divisible by 3 if r is an integer. Here's why: if r is an integer, then $6r$ is an integer, and $6r$ definitely has 6 as a factor because it is a multiple of 6. That means that 2 and 3 are also both (prime) factors of $6r$. If 3 is a factor of $6r$, then there is no remainder when it is divided by 3; that is, the remainder is 0.

(1) This is what we needed to know. The remainder would be 0 for any value of *r* when it is divided by 3, as discussed above. Sufficient.

(2) This means that *r* could be an integer, such as 4, giving us a remainder of 0, OR *r* could be a fraction, such as $\frac{4}{3}$, meaning that $6r$ is 8. In that case, 8 divided by 3 has a remainder of 2. Insufficient.

30. **(B)**

Solution: The value of the expression can be found by changing three separate fractions into one. It can be converted as follows: $\frac{1}{0.03} + \frac{1}{0.37}$ can be changed to one fraction by finding a common denominator (the product of 0.03 and 0.37).

$$\frac{1}{0.03} + \frac{1}{0.37} = \frac{0.37}{0.03(0.37)} + \frac{0.03}{0.37(0.03)} = \frac{0.37 + 0.03}{(0.03)(0.37)} = \frac{0.4}{(0.03)(0.37)} = \frac{0.4}{0.0111}$$

Substitute this into the equation to derive the following:

$$\frac{1}{\frac{1}{0.03} + \frac{1}{0.37}} = \frac{1}{\frac{0.4}{0.0111}} = \frac{0.0111}{0.4} = 0.02775. \text{ Therefore, the answer is B.}$$

31. **(B)**

It first must be noted that the interior angles of an equilateral triangle are all 60 degrees, and that the area of a triangle is $\frac{1}{2}$ (base · height). The uniqueness of a 30-60-90 triangle can be found in the Veritas Geometry Manual. The area of region BCDE can be found by subtracting the area of ΔABE from the area of ΔACD. Since ACD is equilateral, an altitude to its base divides the triangle into two identical right triangles with acute angles of 30 and 60 degrees. Since the hypotenuse of each right triangle is 3 and the base is $\frac{3}{2}$, the altitude can be calculated with the Pythagorean Theorem or with the knowledge of 30-60-90 triangles: It is equal to $\frac{3}{2}\sqrt{3}$. Therefore, the area of ΔACD is $\frac{1}{2}(3)\left(\frac{3\sqrt{3}}{2}\right) = \frac{9}{4}\sqrt{3}$. Since right ΔABE is also a 30-60-90 triangle, AB = 1, AE = 2(1) and BE = $1\sqrt{3}$.

The area of $\triangle ABE$ is $\frac{1}{2}(1)(\sqrt{3}) = \frac{\sqrt{3}}{2}$.

Therefore, the area of region BCDE is $\frac{9}{4}\sqrt{3} - \frac{1}{2}(\sqrt{3}) = \frac{7}{4}\sqrt{3}$, and the answer is B.

32. (E)

Having decimals in a fraction makes it difficult. Multiplying both the numerator and the

denominator by 10,000 can remove the decimals, and yields $\dfrac{250 \cdot \frac{15}{2} \cdot 48}{5 \cdot 24 \cdot \frac{3}{4}}$

Simplifying the numerator and denominator further yields

$$\frac{250 \cdot 15 \cdot \frac{48}{2}}{5 \cdot \frac{24}{4} \cdot 3} = \frac{250 \cdot 15 \cdot 24}{5 \cdot 6 \cdot 3} = 1,000$$

Thus, the answer is E.

33. (A)

If c is the number of correct answers, the number of incorrect answers is $(22 - c)$ and the

test score can be used to form an equation, as follows:

$3.5c - 1(22 - c) = 63.5$ (distribute the -1)

$3.5c - 22 + c = 63.5$ (isolate the numbers and variables)

$4.5c = 85.5$ (divide both sides by 4.5)

$c = 19$ (substitute into the expression for incorrect answers)

Incorrect answers - $(22 - c) = (22 - 19) = 3$

Thus, the number of incorrect answers is 3, and the answer is A.

34. (E)

To calculate the total area, the rectangular parking lot must be added to the attached

semicircle minus the shaded area.

The area of the rectangular section is $30 \cdot 40 = 1,200$.

Since the area of a semicircle is $\frac{1}{2}(\pi)r^2$, the large semicircular area is $\frac{1}{2} \cdot \pi \cdot 20^2$.

The shaded area, also semicircular, is $\frac{1}{2} \cdot \pi \cdot 10^2 = 50\pi$.

Thus, the total area of the lot, excluding the shaded part, is 1,200 + 200π - 50π = 1,200 + 150π. Therefore, the answer is E.

35. **(C)**

If 15 of the switches are defective, then 20%, or 20 out of each 100 switches , are defective. Of that group, 4/5 are rejected, which means that, out of every 100 total switches, 16 are both defective and rejected. Of the 80 nondefective switches, 1/4 are accidentally rejected, which means that 20 are accidentally rejected. Accordingly, there are 16 defective and 20 nondefective switches rejected out of each group of 100, for a total of 36 rejected switches, and 64 that are not rejected, and therefore sold. Of that group of 64 switches sold, the 4 defective switches that were not rejected remain. Therefore, the percentage of switches sold that are defective can be calculated as the 4 defective switches sold divided by the 64 total switches sold: 4/64 * 100% = 6.25%, and the correct answer is C.

36. **(C)**

To solve this problem, it is a good idea to draw out the figure quickly using your understanding of coordinate geometry. Once you can see the basics of the figure, you must determine the necessary dimensions to solve for the area of the trapezoid.

Remember: Area of Trapezoid = (Average of the Parallel Sides)(Height)

The parallel lines of the trapezoid are the two lines $y = 0$ and $y = 4$. The height should be clear as it is the distance between those lines which is simply 4 - 0 or 4. To finish the problem you need to get the length of each of the parallel segments and then take the average of them. To determine the length of the segment on $y = 0$ you need the x intercepts of the two non-parallel lines. Those are 1 and 10 so the length of the bottom segment is 10 -1 or 9. To calculate the intersection points of those two lines on $y = 4$ either reason it out with your understanding of slope or solve for the intersection points by using the two equations.

If $y = 4$ and $y = x - 1$

then the point of intersection is (5,4)

If $y = 4$ and $y = -2x + 20$ then the point

of intersection is (8,4)

The difference between the x coordinates is the length

of the top segment which is 8 − 5 or 3.

The area of the trapezoid is then $\left(\dfrac{9+3}{2}\right)(4) = 24$ Answer is C.

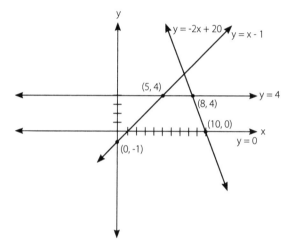

37. **(D)**

Reference the Veritas Problem Solving Manual for assistance with permutation and combination problems.

Each family must be kept together, so there are N! ways that the families (as units) can be arranged. Within each family, there are M members, so there are M! ways that the members of each individual

family can be arranged. For each arrangement of one family, there are M! arrangements of each of the other families, or M! · (M!$^{N-1}$) or M!^{N}.

Hence, the final answer is N! · M!^{N}, and the answer is D.

38. **(D)**

The prime factorization of 343 is $7 \cdot 7 \cdot 7$. This means that r, s, and t could be, in any order: 1, 1, and 343; 1, 7, and 49; or 7, 7, and 7. Those are the only three possibilities.

(1) This means that r, s, and t must be 1, 7, and 49, in that order. t is therefore 49. Sufficient.

(2) This means that r is 1 and s is 7 or the other way around. In either case, t is 49. Sufficient.

39. **(C)**

This problem requires a bit of logic, and an understanding of permutations from the Veritas Problem Solving Manual. For the first country, Arne has 13 options.

For the second country, Arne has only 12 options, because one is already taken and can not be repeated.

In each country, there are 4 options, so, the results are as follows:

airports for first destination: $13 \cdot 4$

airports for second destination: $12 \cdot 4$

Note that $_{13}P_2 = \dfrac{13!}{(13-2)!} = \dfrac{13!}{11!} = 13 \cdot 12$

Therefore, the total number of flight paths is

$13 \cdot 4 \cdot 12 \cdot 4 = 13 \cdot 12 \cdot 4^2$

Thus, the answer is C.

40. **(D)**

Solution: It is easiest in this situation to visualize the number of options in which Earl is NOT sitting between friends and subsequently subtracting this number from the total number of seat arrangements.

Since the friends can sit together in 5! ways, 5! is the total number of seat arrangements. Earl can sit on the far right side in 4! ways and on the far left side in 4! ways. So Earl can sit in among the middle three friends in $5! - 4! - 4! = 120 - 24 - 24 = 72$ ways.

Therefore, the correct answer is D.

41. **(C)**

Joe's earnings for driving 525 miles is calculated by combining his earnings for driving 300 miles and his earnings for driving 225 extra miles. Since he is paid 45 cents per mile for the first 300 miles and 20 cents extra for each additional mile, he earns (300 miles · $0.45) = $135 for the first 300 miles, and

(225 miles · $0.65) = $146.25 for additional miles.

The sum of $135 and $146.25 is $281.25; therefore, Joe's total earnings for the day is $281.25, and the answer is C.

42. **(B)**

In data set I there is no variation, so the standard deviation is 0.

Data set III has small variations from the mean of 53 (increments of 1), so the standard deviation is greater in III than in I.

In data set II, because of the extreme values of 36 and 71, the variation in the set is clearly greater than the variation in III.

Thus, the standard deviation of 0 in I is smaller than the standard deviation in III, which is smaller than the standard deviation in II.

Therefore, the answer is B.

43. **(B)**

If there are x CDs in the store, $\left(\frac{1}{6} + \frac{1}{3} + \frac{1}{4}\right)x$ or $\frac{3}{4}x$ of the CDs are rock, pop, or classical. This leaves $\left(\frac{1}{4}\right)x$ or 15 CDs that are alternative.

Thus, $\left(\frac{1}{4}\right)x = 15$, where, after multiplying both sides by 4, $x = 60$. Thus, the answer is B.

44. **(C)**

The sum of the 16 scores is $16 \cdot 62.5 = 1000.0$.

The sum of the remaining 15 scores is $15 \cdot 64.0 = 960.0$.

Finding the difference between the two results in the score of the student who dropped the class: $1000.0 - 960.0 = 40.0$. Thus, the answer is C.

45. (C)

This problem should be approached like any other equality or inequality comparing two figures, and x should be determined in the simplest form possible.

If $0 < 3x + 3 < 48$, then subtracting 3 from each of the three parts of the inequality yields $-3 < 3x < 45$.

Subsequently, dividing all parts of the inequality by 3 yields $-1 < x < 15$.

The 15 integers that satisfy this inequality are 0 through 14; therefore, the answer is C.

46. (D)

Mr. Goldstein's sales tax can be calculated by multiplying the sales tax by the price of the vehicle after subtracting out what he was able to negotiate for a discount. The amount he pays for sales tax is

$(0.05)[(\$45,500)(0.8)] = \$1,820$.

Thus, the answer is d).

47. (A)

For a number to be a multiple of 14, it must have 2 and 7 as prime factors. For a number to be a multiple of 21, it needs to have 3 and 7 as prime factors. Therefore, the smallest multiple of 14 that is also a multiple of 21 is $2 \cdot 7 \cdot 3$. The next multiple of 14 is $2 \cdot 7 \cdot 4$. This is not a multiple of 21, however, since it does not have 3 as a factor. The next multiple of 14 is $2 \cdot 7 \cdot 5$, also not a multiple of 21 since it lacks a 3 as a factor. The next multiple of 14 is $2 \cdot 7 \cdot 6$, which does have a 3 as a factor, so it is a multiple of 21 as well. The next common multiple of 14 and 21 is $2 \cdot 7 \cdot 9$, and then $2 \cdot 7 \cdot 12$. In other words, 1 out of every 3 multiples of 14 is also a multiple of 21, or one-third of 14's multiples are also 21's multiples.

(1) One-third of 30 is 10, so there are 10 multiples in this set that are also multiples of 21. Sufficient.

(2) We don't know if Set T has 1 member, 100 members, 1,000 members, or any other

number of members. Insufficient.

48. **(A)**

Average weight, in pounds per cake, is equal to the total weight divided by the number of cakes.

The total number of cakes is a + b, and their total weight is the weight of each cake times the number of cakes: $4a + 7b$. Therefore, the average weight per cake is $\frac{4a + 7b}{a + b}$, and the answer is A.

49. **(C)**

One approach is to express the left side of each of the choices in terms of $\frac{x}{y}$. Thus, a) is true since

$\frac{x + y}{y} = \frac{x}{y} + 1 = \frac{4}{5} + 1 = \frac{9}{5}$. Choices d) and e) can be shown to be true in a similar manner.

One way to see that b) is true is to first invert both sides, that is, show that $\frac{y-x}{y} = \frac{1}{5}$. This is true since $\frac{y-x}{y} = \frac{y}{y} - \frac{x}{y} = 1 - \frac{4}{5} = \frac{1}{5}$. On the other hand, c) is not true since $\frac{x-y}{y} = \frac{x}{y} - 1 = \frac{4}{5} - 1$

$= -\frac{1}{5} \neq \frac{1}{5}$.

Alternatively, since $\frac{x}{y} = \frac{4}{5}$, it can be assumed that x = 4 and y = 5 (or some multiple of those numbers), and each variable can be plugged in and checked. For instance, choice c) is $\frac{4 - 5}{5}$

$\neq \frac{1}{5}$, therefore, the correct answer is C.

50. **(E)**

Since a and b are not both even, either one or both of them is odd. To determine if the answer choice is odd, each choice can be checked for both cases as shown in the table below .

	Both Odd	**One Even and One Odd**
ab	Odd	Even
a + b	Even	Odd
a – b	Even	Odd

$a + b - 1$	Odd	Even
$2(a + b) - 1$	Odd	Odd

Since the correct answer must be odd, any even result eliminates an answer choice.

Choices $a - d$ can all be even. $2(a + b) - 1$ is the only one of the expressions that must be odd in both cases, so the answer is E.

51. (E)

The average of 10, 12, and 14 is $\frac{10 + 12 + 14}{3} = 12$, which equals the average of

9, 11, and x. Thus, $\frac{9 + 11 + x}{3} = 12$ (multiply both sides by 3) $\rightarrow$

$20 + x = 36$ (subtract 20 from both sides) $\rightarrow x = 16$. Thus, the answer is E.

52. (B)

Let m represent the number of miles that John runs. On the uphill trip, John took $\frac{m}{5}$ hours, and on the trip downhill, John took $\frac{m}{7}$ hours.

Hence, the average speed for John's run is the total number of miles, or 2m divided by the total time, or $\frac{m}{5} + \frac{m}{7}$.

Thus, the average speed is $\frac{2m}{\frac{m}{5} + \frac{m}{7}} = \frac{2}{\frac{1}{5} + \frac{1}{7}} = \frac{2}{\frac{12}{35}} = \frac{70}{12}$, which is approximately 5.83 miles per hour.

Thus, the answer is B.

53. (D)

To calculate how many miles from Portland Ann and Bill will meet, first find their combined speed, which is $50 + 70 = 120$ miles per hour. Since the distance between the two cities is 200 miles, they travel for

$\frac{200}{120} = 1.67$ hours, which is how long it will take them to meet.

Then, to calculate how many miles from Portland Ann drives before she meets Bill, multiply this by her average speed: $1.67 \cdot 50 = 83.3$ miles. Thus, the answer is D.

54. (B)

First, it must be understood that the average of three numbers, *m*, *n*, and *p* is $\frac{m+n+p}{3}$.

Since $11m - n = p$, or $n + p = 11m$, substituting $11m$ for $n + p$ results in $\frac{(11m) + m}{3} = \frac{12m}{3} =$

$4m$. Thus, the answer is b).

55. (E)

The trick to this problem is realizing that both the original number of cases and the new

number of cases have to be whole numbers.

We know an obvious scenario that would fit this description would be if the original

number were 100 and the final number were 185 (100 · 0.85 = 85). However, the answer

choices are all less than this.

Therefore, reduce 100 and 85 by the same factor until they cannot be reduced further.

$\frac{100}{5} = 20$ and $\frac{85}{5} = 17$

Therefore, the answer is E.

56. (E)

(1) This tells us that $\sqrt{7ab} = \sqrt{49b} = 7\sqrt{b}$. We have no idea what *b* is. Insufficient.

(2) This tells us nothing about *a*. Insufficient.

Together, we have $7\sqrt{b}$, and we know that *b* is the cube of some integer. If *b* were 8 (which

is 2^3), then the answer is NO, this is not an integer. If *b* were 64 (4^3) then the answer is YES,

since $7\sqrt{64} = 7 \cdot 8 = 56$, an integer. Thus, since we said both YES and NO, together the state-

ments are still insufficient.

57. (E)

The average number of cookies sold per day, per "good" day, and per "fair" day were 820,

980, and 640, respectively.

If *g* represents the number of "good" days and f represents the number of "fair" days, then

$980g + 640f = 820(g + f)$, which yields $160g = 180f \rightarrow 8g = 9f$

Hence, $\frac{g}{f} = \frac{9}{8}$; therefore, the ratio of the number of "good" days to the number of "fair" days is 9 to 8. Thus, the answer is E.

58. (A)

Average score $= \frac{\text{Total Score}}{\text{\# of Games}}$. For the first m miles, the racehorse ran a total of rm miles, and for the final race, the horse ran n miles. This results in total number of $rm + n$ miles.

The total number of races the horse ran would be $r + 1$.

The average number of miles run for the $r + 1$ races is $\frac{rm + n}{r + 1}$ miles.

Thus, the answer is A.

59. (D)

Let m be the number of $10 bills that were used and let n be the number of $50 bills that were used.

Then $m + n = 15$, and either $m = n + 1$ or $m = n - 1$.

Thus, either m = 8 and $n = 7$, or m = 7 and $n = 8$.

In the first case, the amount of lost money would have been $1,200 - m(\$10) - n(\$50)$

$= \$1,200 - \$80 - \$350 = \$770$; whereas, in the second case, the value would have been

$1,200 - $70 - $400 = $730. Since the lesser of these amounts is $730, the answer is d).

Alternatively, note that the minimum possible amount of lost money corresponds to the

maximum possible value of the bills that were spent. This would require as many $50 bills

to be spent as possible, where $m = 7$ and $n = 8$, and the amount of lost money is $1,200 -

$70 - $400 = $730.

60. (C)

Since 50 percent of the books that were borrowed during the week were not returned to

the library on or before Saturday morning, you can subtract half the number borrowed

from 40 to get the remaining books: $40 - .5x =$ at least 22, where x is the number bor-

rowed. Since we want the greatest number of different books that could have been lent

out during the week, we want the least number of books on the shelves on Saturday morning. Then 40 - .5x = exactly 22. Thus .5x = 18, and x = 36.

Thus, the answer is C.

61. **(B)**

If x is the fifth profit and the average profit is $220, then the sum of all the profits divided by the number of profits must equal $\frac{300 + 140 + 60 + 270 + x}{5} = 220$

(multiply both sides by 5) $\rightarrow$ 300 + 140 + 60 + 270 + x = 1100

(sum all numbers) $\rightarrow$ 770 + x = 1100

(subtract 770 from both sides) $\rightarrow$ x = 330

Thus, the answer is B.

62. **(D)**

If 85 percent of the sales came from selling paintings, then the remaining 15 percent, totaling $330,000, came from selling sculptures. If s represents total sales, then 0.15r = $330,000 and r = $2,200,000.

Thus, the answer is D.

63. **(C)**

Let A and B represent the capacities of buckets A and B, respectively.

The amount of water in bucket A is $\frac{1}{4}$A and the amount of water in bucket B is $\frac{3}{4}$.

Since the capacity of bucket B is three times the capacity of bucket A, it follows that B = 3A, or A = $\frac{1}{3}$B , and the water in bucket A is $\frac{1}{4}$A = $\frac{1}{12}$B .

When the water in bucket A is poured into bucket B, B contains $\frac{1}{12}$B + $\frac{3}{4}$B = $\frac{5}{6}$B , which is $\frac{5}{6}$ of its capacity. Thus, the answer is C.

64. **(E)**

If b represents the number of *Salmonella* bacteria, then $4b$ represents the number of *E. Coli* bacteria, and $b + 4b$ represents the total bacterial population.

Thus, the ratio of the *E. Coli* bacteria to the total population is $\frac{4b}{b+4b} = \frac{4b}{5b} = \frac{4}{5}$ or 4 to 5.

Thus, the answer is E.

65. (E)

(1) Given this information, ab would be prime if b is 1, but not prime if b is 2. Insufficient.

(2) Given this information, a could be 7 and b could be 1 (not a prime, don't forget!), making $ab = 7$, a prime. Or a could be 7 and b could be 0.5, making $ab = 3.5$, which is not a prime. Insufficient.

The two examples given in the explanation above for Statement 2 prove that even with a as a prime and b not a prime, the answer to this question could be YES or NO. Thus, the statements are insufficient together.

66. (E)

The malfunctioning machine increases the number of defects by $110 - 60 = 50$.

Therefore, the increase in number of defects can be calculated as a percent if the change is divided by the original number of defects: $\frac{50}{60} = \frac{5}{6} = 83\frac{1}{3}\%$.

Thus, the answer is E.

67. (B)

First, the travel time has to be calculated by dividing distance by rate: $\frac{1950 \text{ miles}}{650 \frac{\text{miles}}{\text{hour}}} = 3$ hours.

The plane is scheduled to arrive in Denver at 2 AM Denver time or 4 AM Boston time. 3 hours before 4 AM is 1 AM Boston time.

Thus, the answer is B.

68. **(D)**

Having the used DVD player repaired will cost $36.00 for 2 years, which translates to an

average cost of $\frac{\$36.00}{2} = \$18.00$ per year. The new DVD player cost $90.00 for 4 years,

which comes out to an average of $\frac{\$90.00}{4} = \$22.50$ per year, or $4.50 greater per year than

the cost of repairing the used DVD player.

To calculate the percentage, divide the difference by the cost of repairing the used DVD

player:

$\frac{\$4.50}{\$18.00} = 25\%$ greater than the cost of repairing the used DVD player.

Thus, the answer is D.

69. **(D)**

If t represents the number of tiles in the left-most row, the number of tiles in the next

eight rows are

$t - 2, t - 4, t - 6, t - 8, t - 10, t - 12, t - 14$, and $t - 16$, respectively.

The total number of tiles in the nine rows is $t + (t - 2) + (t - 4) + (t - 6) + (t - 8) + (t - 10) +$

$(t - 12) + (t - 14) + (t - 16) = 9t - 72 = 504$.

Since $9t - 72 = 504$, $9t = 576$, and $t = 64$.

Thus, the answer is D.

70. **(A)**

The average speed, in miles per hour, for the entire trip is equal to the total distance in

miles

$(k + 300)$ divided by the total time in hours, $\left(\frac{96 + t}{60}\right)$ or $\frac{k + 300}{\frac{96 + t}{60}}$.

The division can be simplified by multiplying both the numerator and denominator by 60

and obtaining

$\frac{60(k + 300)}{96 + t}$.

Thus, the answer is A.

71. (E)

Since George receives a commission of $15 plus a 20 percent commission on total rental fees, his commission for that week was the flat rate commission of $15 on 50 costumes, plus 20 percent of the total rental price, $7,950.

The calculations are below:

$50(\$15) + (0.2)(\$7,950) = \$2,340$

Thus, the answer is E.

72. (C)

To answer this question, do a factor tree to determine the possible factors of 595.
$595 \rightarrow 119 \rightarrow 17$
$\quad \downarrow \qquad \downarrow$
$\quad 5 \qquad 7$

Since 35 has the factors 5 and 7, b) cannot be the correct answer. Similarly, 85 has the factors 5 and 17, and 119 has the factors 7 and 17, and therefore neither d) nor e) are correct. Thus, the answer is C.

73. (D)

At 9:00 a.m., there are nine tolls of the bell that last for three seconds each, which means that there are $9 \cdot 3 = 27$ seconds total for all of the tolls combined. Since there are eight intervals of silence, lasting for two seconds each, between the nine tolls, the silences last for $8 \cdot 2 = 16$ seconds combined. Thus, the total time elapsed between the beginning of the first toll and the end of the last toll at 9:00 a.m. is
$27 + 16 = 43$ seconds. Thus, the answer is D.

74. (A)

C must be 1 or 2, since it's impossible to add a two-digit number (*AB*) to a number that is less than 200 (1*AB*) and get a number that it is more than 298.

(1) C must be 1. The most that A could be is 4. The most that B could be is 9. This still means that C is 1. Sufficient.

(2) B could be 9 and A could be 8. In this case, C is 2. Or B could be 9 and A could be 1. In that case, C is 1. Insufficient.

75. **(B)**

If Georgia loses 9 individual gloves, they could belong to 5, 6, 7, 8, or 9 different pairs of gloves. Therefore, the greatest possible number of pairs of matched gloves is 13 – 5 = 8. Alternatively, assuming that all the gloves are identical (even though the problem states that they come in different patterns), there were originally 26 gloves altogether, and after the loss, there are 26 – 9 = 17 gloves left. This could at most be 8 pairs.

Thus, the answer is B.

76. **(E)**

The number of minutes it takes to travel 180 miles at 600 miles per hour can be found by dividing the distance by the rate.

However, dimensional analysis is needed to adjust the units:

$$\frac{180 \text{miles} \cdot 60 \frac{\text{minutes}}{\text{hour}}}{600 \frac{\text{miles}}{\text{hour}}} = 18 \text{ minutes.}$$ Thus, the answer is E.

77. **(C)**

The problem states that in the United States last year, 390 people out of each 100,000 suffered from a myocardial infarction. This fraction, when multiplied by the total number of people living in the U.S. last year, yields the number of myocardial infarctions. The only difficulty arises in the units. Since 350 million is equal to 3,500 · 100,000, the number of people that suffered from myocardial infarctions last year was

$$\frac{390}{100,000} \cdot (3,500 \cdot 100,000) = 390 \cdot 3,500 = 1,365,000 \text{ people.}$$

Thus, the answer is C.

78. **(A)**

A number that is divisible by 4, 5, 6, and 7 must contain these numbers as factors.

Because 4 contains 2 factors of 2, and 6 contains only one factor of 2, the number must contain a second factor of 2.

The number is $(2)(5)(6)(7) = 420$.

Alternatively, this answer can also be achieved by the "guess and check" method. Try to fit each factor into the answer choice, knowing the above assumptions.

Thus, the answer is A.

79. **(A)**

If 40 percent of the members of the accounting association have passed the CPA exam, then 60 percent have not. Among the members who have not passed the test, 50 work at an accounting firm and 55 are in school, for a total of 105 members.

If x represents the number of members in the accounting association, $0.60x = 105$, and thus, $x = 175$.

Thus, the answer is A.

80. **(D)**

This problem can be solved by finding the difference between the total number of two-element subsets and the number of subsets that contain both 5 and 7. There is only one two-element subset that contains both 5 and 7. The total number of two-element subsets is $\frac{(5)(4)}{2} = 10$, because there are 5 options for the first element, and 4 remain for the second element. The reason that the product is divided by 2 is to remove subsets with orders rearranged, because {4,5} is the same as {5,4}.

The difference between 10 and 1 is 9.

Alternatively, the two element subsets of {4,5,6,7,8} can be listed:

{4,5}, {4,6}, {4,7}, {4,8}, {5,6}, {5,8}, {6,7}, {6,8}, and {7,8}.

There are 9 two-element subsets that do not contain both 5 and 7.

Thus, the answer is D.

81. **(E)**

Note that each column contains six 1's, six 2's, six 5's, and six 7's,

whose sum is $6(1 + 2 + 5 + 7) = 6(15) = 90$.

In the tens, hundreds, and thousands columns, the sum is 99 due to the 9 carried from the

previous column.

Therefore, the sum of these 24 integers is 99,990.

Thus, the answer is E.

82. **(D)**

This should be converted into a fraction and then simplified:

$\frac{16}{40} = \frac{4}{10} \rightarrow \frac{40}{100}$ or $0.40 = 40\%$.

Thus, the answer is D.

83. **(E)**

(1) This only tells us that the average of these three numbers is c, but we don't have a value

for c. Insufficient. (2) This does not tell us anything about a. Insufficient.

Together, Statement 1 told us that the average of the three numbers is c but Statement 2

does not provide enough information to determine the value of c. Insufficient.

84. **(B)**

On the 5-day camping trip, each adult consumed an average of $\frac{\$90}{3}$ or \$30 worth of

freeze-dried meals. Thus, the cost of meals per person per day was $\frac{\$30}{5}$ days= \$6.

At the same rate, the cost of meals consumed by 8 adults during a 9-day camping trip

would be $9(8)(\$6) = \$432$. Thus, the answer is B.

85. **(C)**

The number of dentists who responded to the poll was 0.3(88,000) = 26,400.

If 15 percent of the respondents declared a preference for Y, then 85 percent did not declare a preference for Y. Multiplying the number of respondents by the percentage of respondents that did not state their preference will yield the number of respondents without a preference for Y: (0.85)(26,400) = 22,440. Thus, the answer is C.

86. **(E)**

If each fraction is written in decimal form, finding the sum is easy:

$$\begin{array}{r} 0.02 \\ 0.004 \\ + \, 0.00006 \\ \hline 0.02406 \end{array}$$

Thus, the answer is E.

87. **(B)**

The prime factorization of 1,155 is (3)(5)(7)(11). (To determine this, it might be helpful to divide 1155 by a very simple factor, 5. The remainder is 231, which is divisible by 3. Then the remainder becomes 77, which is divisible only by 7 and 11.)

Since $a > b > c > d > 1$ and the variables are integers, the values for the variables must be $a = 11, b = 7, c = 5$, and $d = 3$, so $a - d = 11 - 3 = 8$.

Thus, the answer is B.

88. **(A)**

Since there is one vehicle accident every 45 seconds, there are 4 accidents every 180 seconds, or 3 minutes: $\dfrac{1 \text{ accident}}{45 \text{ seconds}} \cdot \dfrac{4}{4} = \dfrac{4 \text{ accidents}}{180 \text{ seconds}}$

Thus, in 2 hours, the number of accidents that occurs is:

120 minutes $\cdot \dfrac{4 \text{ accidents}}{3 \text{ minutes}} = 160$ accidents.

Thus, the answer is A.

89. **(D)**

In order to answer this problem, a thorough understanding of the operations must be possessed. Each value should be calculated independently, and the difference should be determined.

-10 – (-5) is equivalent to -10 + 5 = -5

-5 – (-10) is equivalent to -5 + 10 = 5

The difference between -5 and 5 is 5 – (-5) = 10

Thus, the value of the first expression is 10 less than the value of the second, and the answer is D.

90. **(C)**

To determine the least possible number of tennis balls needed, the smallest possible number of balls should be placed in each bucket, subject to the constraints of the problem. Thus, one ball should be placed in five of the buckets, 2 balls in the sixth bucket, 3 balls in the seventh, 4 balls in the eighth, and 5 balls in the ninth. The least possible number of tennis balls is therefore 1 + 1 + 1 + 1 + 1 + 2 + 3 + 4 + 5 = 19. Thus, the answer is C.

91. **(B)**

If the Tax Preparers work a 12 hour workday, Tax Preparer A can prepare $\frac{x}{12 \text{ hours}} = \frac{16 \text{ returns}}{8 \text{ hours}}$, so $x = 24$ returns. Tax Preparer B can prepare $\frac{y}{12 \text{ hours}} = \frac{12 \text{ returns}}{8 \text{ hours}}$, so $y = 18$ returns. Therefore, Tax Preparer A can make $24 \cdot \$75 = \$1800$, and Tax Preparer B can make $18 \cdot \$90 = \$1620$. The difference between the two amounts is $\$1800 - \$1620 = \$180$. Thus, Tax Preparer A can make $180 more than Tax Preparer B if they both work a 12 hour workday, and the answer is B.

92. **(C)**

Liv received $ap + 550s$, since the average price of an item times the number of items sold equals the total amount of money received from the sale of the items.

(1) This tells us that Liv received $1,650 ($550 · 3) for the sculptures, but tells us nothing about a or p. Insufficient.

(2) This tells us nothing about s, just that the average price per painting multiplied by the number of paints sold is $2,200. Insufficient.

Together we know that Liv received $2,200 + $1,650 = $3,850. Sufficient.

93. (E)

The number of Stereo ys sold was $\frac{2}{3}(720)= 480$, so the number of Stereo xs sold was $720 - 480 = 240$.

Since the price of Stereo x is $540 and this is 60 percent of the price of Stereo y, the price of Stereo y is $\frac{\$540}{0.6} = \$900$. Thus, the total revenue from the sales of the stereos is:

$240(\$540) + 480(\$900) = \$129,600 + \$432,000 = \$561,600$.

Thus, the answer is E.

94. (E)

This problem requires the "guess and check" method, with which different combinations can be tried on each answer choice. For each of choices a) through D, there is a combination of the packages that gives that total:

a) $9 = 1 + 3 + 5$

b) $10 = 3 + 7$

c) $12 = 5 + 7$

d) $13 = 1 + 5 + 7$

However, no combination of the packages adds up to a total of 14 cookies, since the total number of the four different packages is $1 + 3 + 5 + 7 = 16$ cookies, and there is no combination of packages with only 2 cookies, whose removal would result in a combination with 14 cookies. Thus, the answer is E.

95. (E)

If $\sqrt{x} > 16$, then $x > 16^2$.

Hence, $\frac{x}{16} > \frac{16^2}{16}$ or $\frac{x}{16} > 16$.

Since only choice e) is greater than 16, the answer is E.

96. **(D)**

The calculations below give the distribution of Frank's earnings of $42,000:

Rental expenses: $\frac{1}{3}$ ($42,000) = $14,000

Food: $\frac{2}{5}$ ($42,000 - $14,000) = $11,200

Utilities and miscellaneous expenses: $\frac{1}{4}$ ($42,000) = $10,500

Savings: $42,000 – ($14,000 + $11,200 + $10,500) = $6,300

Therefore, Frank put $6,300 into savings, and the answer is D.

97. **(A)**

The sum of the three numbers in the vertical column is 56 + 39 + 61 = 156.

The product of the three numbers in the horizontal row is 39ab.

Thus, 39ab = 156 → ab = 4

Thus, the answer is A.

98. **(B)**

The ratio of the charge per minute for a call placed during December to the charge per minute for a call placed during May is $\frac{\$3.00}{\$4.50}$ or $\frac{2}{3}$.

Therefore, if the charge for a call placed during May is $36.00, the charge for a call of the same duration placed during December would be $\frac{2}{3}$ ($36.00) = $24.00.

Thus, the answer is B.

99. **(E)**

The percent decrease in the price of an item = $\frac{the\ decrease\ in\ the\ cost\ of\ the\ item}{the\ original\ price\ of\ the\ item}$.

Thus, the percent decrease in the price of a hardcover book is $\frac{(24.95 - 9.95)}{24.95}$, or $\frac{15}{24.95}$, which is a little more than $\frac{15}{25}$, or 60 percent.

 Thus, the answer is E.

100. **(B)**

Since the ratio of flour to butter to eggs is 7 : 4 : 2, for each 7 + 4 + 2, or 13, equal parts by weight of the recipe, 7 parts are flour and 2 parts are eggs.

There are then $\frac{7}{13}$ (65) = 35 pounds of flour and $\frac{2}{13}$ (65) = 10 pounds of eggs.

Therefore, there are 35 − 10 = 25 pounds more of flour than eggs in 65 pounds of the recipe. Alternatively, it is clear in the problem that 13 pounds of the recipe contains 7 pounds of flour and 2 pounds of eggs. Sixty-five pounds is 5 times that size, or 5 · 13. The quantities of ingredients can then be multiplied by 5.

Flour becomes 7 · 5 = 35 pounds.

Eggs become 2 · 5 = 10 pounds.

The difference is 25 pounds.

Thus, the answer is B.

101. **(A)**

(1) Since the y-coordinate of point A is 3, the distance from A straight down to the x-axis is 3. If we draw a line segment from A to (0, 0), we'll have formed the hypotenuse of a right triangle. We can then use the Pythagorean Theorem to find the distance from (0, 0). This will be the *x*-coordinate of point A. Of course, we don't really need to do this, but we could if we wanted to. Sufficient. (2) As in the explanation to Statement 1, since the *y*-coordinate of point A is 3, the distance from A straight down to the *x*-axis is 3. If you draw a line segment from A to(3, 0), we'll have formed the hypotenuse of a right triangle. We can then use the Pythagorean Theorem to find the length of the short leg. This is the distance from (3, 0), (which happens to be 0.5, though you don't need to perform the calculations to obtain this value). However, knowing the length of the sides of this triangle still does not give us the x-coordinate of point A, since we don't know if point A is located to the left or

to the right of the *x*-coordinate (3, 0).Insufficient.

NOTE: Drawing diagrams would aid in understanding why Statement 2 is insufficient.

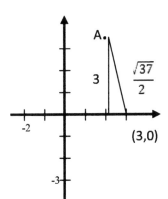
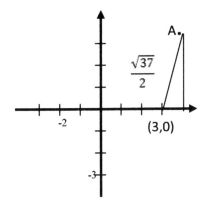

102. **(B)**

For assistance with parentheses, refer to the Veritas Algebra Book.

In this problem every term in one set of parentheses needs to be multiplied by every term

in the other set of parentheses: $(2 + \sqrt{3})(2 - \sqrt{3}) = 2^2 + 2\sqrt{3} - 2\sqrt{3} - (\sqrt{3})^2 \rightarrow = 4 - (\sqrt{3})^2 =$

$4 - 3 = 1$

Thus, the answer is B.

103. **(C)**

If the population of insects doubles every 20 days, it doubles 15 times in 300 days.

The population after 20 days was $2(10^3)$, and after 40 days was $(2)(2)(10^3)$, or $(22)(10^3)$. Continuing to multiply by 2 each time the population doubles, it follows that the population

after 300 days is $(2^{15})(10^3)$.

Thus, the answer is C.

104. **(C)**

To calculate the revenue, the price of each item needs to be multiplied by the number sold. If the price of a pair of jeans is $150, then the number x of jeans that would be sold is:

$x = 1300 - 6(150) = 400$ pairs. Thus, the total revenue from the sale of 400 pairs of jeans at $150 each would be $150(400) = $60,000$.

Thus, the answer is C.

105. **(A)**

One way to solve problems of this type is to construct a Venn diagram and to assign values to the non-overlapping regions. For example,

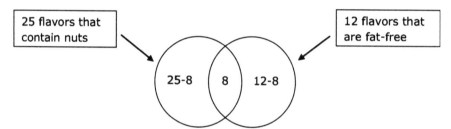

If there were 35 flavors in all, then the number of flavors that are neither fat-free nor have nuts is

$35 - (17 + 8 + 4) = 6$.

Thus, the answer is A.

106. **(C)**

If r represents the revenue during the third quarter, then 132 percent of r represents the revenue earned during the fourth quarter, or $1.32r = \$3,564,000$, and $r = \dfrac{\$3,564,000}{1.32} = \$2,700,000$.

Thus, the answer is C.

107. **(C)**

Since 3 and 13 are both prime numbers, if x is divisible by both, then x must also be divisible by $3(13) = 39$. Thus, x is of the form $39y$, where y is some integer.

Thus, the answer is C.

108. **(D)**

If the music artist's song played on the radio x times, then he received $1.20(50,000) or $60,000 for the first 50,000 times the song plays, and $0.80(x – 50,000) for the rest of the times the song plays on the radio, for a total of $520,000.

This can be combined to form an equation:

$520,000 = $60,000 + $0.80(x – 50,000) $\rightarrow$ $520,000 = $60,000 + $0.80x – $40,000 $\rightarrow$

$520,000 = $20,000 + $0.80x $\rightarrow$ $500,000 = $0.80x

x = 625,000

Thus, the answer is D.

109. **(D)**

An equivalent expression of the inequality is $(n + 1)(n – 1) \geq 0$. The product of the two factors will equal 0 if $n = -1$ or $n = 1$. The product of the two factors will be greater than 0 if both factors are positive or if both factors are negative. In the first case, $n + 1 > 0$ and $n – 1 > 0$, so that $n > -1$ and $n > 1$, or $n > 1$. If both factors are negative, then $n + 1 < 0$ and $n – 1 < 0$, so that $n < 1$ and $n < -1$, or $n < -1$. Therefore, taking all cases into consideration, the solution is $n \leq -1$ or $n \geq 1$. Thus, the answer is D.

110. **(B)**

If the population of the insect colony doubles every two months, then it must now be half of what it will be in two months, or $\frac{3.2 \cdot 10^4}{2} = 1.6 \cdot 10^4$.

Since eight months consists of four 2-month intervals, the population eight months ago was $\left(\frac{1}{2}\right)^4$, or $\frac{1}{16}$ of $1.6 \cdot 10^4$, which would be written in scientific notation, not as $0.1 \cdot 10^4$, but as $1.0 \cdot 10^3$.

Thus, the answer is B.

111. **(D)**

Since y is a prime number greater than 2, y must be odd. The product of two odd numbers must be odd. Therefore, the possible odd divisors of $x = 3y$ are 1, 3, x, and y.

Note: It may be easier to understand this by using an example with actual numbers: e.g., if $y = 7$, then $3y = 21$. Hence, 21 is divisible by 1, 3, 7, and 21.

Thus, the answer is D.

112. **(C)**

To determine which of the statements cannot be true, it may be easiest to consider specific sets of numbers for A and B. For example, suppose A consists of the integers from 1 to 7 and B consists of the same integers except 4. Then, the mean and median of A are both 4, and since the median of B is $\frac{3+5}{2} = 4$, the mean and median of B are both 4 as well. Since the range of a set is the difference between the greatest and smallest numbers in the set, A and B also have the same range, $7 - 1 = 6$. Thus, choices a), d), and e) can be true.

Choice b) can also be true if A is the same as above and B is the set of integers from 1 to 6. The mean of A would be 4, as stated earlier, and the mean of B would be 3.5. To see that choice c) cannot be true, suppose that x denotes the number in A that is not in B. If x is either the smallest or the greatest number in A, then the range of B would be less than the range of A. However, if x is between the smallest number and the greatest number in A, then the range of B would be equal to the range of A.

In any case, the range of A cannot be less than the range of B. The only way this could happen was if B included a number greater than the greatest number in A or smaller than the smallest number in A, both of which are impossible in this scenario.

Thus, the answer is C.

113. **(E)**

Bob spent 2 percent of $75,000 on entertainment expenses, which is $(0.02)(\$75,000) = \$1,500$. Since he put 60 percent of $75,000 in savings, he saved $(0.6)(\$75,000) = \$45,000$. Therefore, he had $\$75,000 - (45,000 + \$1,500) = 28,500$ left over.

Thus, the answer is E.

114. (C)

For assistance with odd and even numbers, refer to the Veritas Arithmetic Book.

Since $ab - a = a(b - 1)$, which is odd, a and $b - 1$ must be both odd.

Therefore, a must be odd and b must be even. Note that answer choices A, B, D, and E must all be even.

Thus, the answer is C.

Challenge Problems

115. (D)

The question stem already gives us one equation: $10b + 8s = 23.90$. Since we have two unknowns, we need two equations to solve for the unknowns. So we now need just one more equation. (1) This tells us that 3 buttons equal $5.25, or $3b = 5.25$. That's our second equation. Sufficient. (2) This tells us that $15b + 13s = 30.00$. That's also a second equation. Sufficient. NOTE: we don't need to actually solve for the cost of one snap; we just need to know that we could do so.

116. (C)

If you have a set of numbers and want to determine the median, arrange them from the lowest number to the highest. The number in the middle is the median. If you have an even number of numbers, as we do here, the median is the average of the middle two numbers. (1) Since the average is equal to the sum of a set of numbers multiplied by the number of numbers in that set, this tells us that the sum of the two unknowns is 616 (308 · 2). However, we still don't know what the unknowns are, so we can't say where they fit in this set of numbers when arranged from lowest to highest. Therefore, we don't know what the median is. Insufficient. (2) The mode is the number that appears most often in a set. This statement tells us that either or both of the unknowns are 0. But this doesn't tell us the value of each unknown by itself. Insufficient. Together, we know that the sum of the unknowns is 616, and one of them is 0. That means the other unknown (we don't know which is which) is 616. We can now arrange the numbers: (-9, 0, 0, 11, 100, 616). Since we have six numbers, the median is the average of 0 and 11, which is 5.5. Sufficient.

117. (C)

(1) This equation, combined with the question stem information, gives us two solutions: $a = 2$ or $a = 0$. Insufficient. (2) This only tells us that a isn't 2. Insufficient. Together, we know that a must be 0, since Statement 2 rules out the possibility that a could be 2. Sufficient.

118. (A)

(1) This translates to $x + x^2 = 12$, which can be arranged into $x^2 + x - 12 = 0$, which can be factored into $(x + 4)(x - 3) = 0$. Thus, x is either $- 4$ or 3. Since neither of these values is greater than 3, the question can be answered with a NO. Sufficient. (2) x could be 4, , which would answer the question with a YES. But x could also be $- 4$, which gives us a NO. Insufficient.

119. (D)

(1) This can be simplified to x < 15. Since the sum of x and y is 23, y must therefore be greater than 8. And since y is an integer, its lowest possible value is 9. This gives us a YES. Sufficient. (2) This allows us to solve for x, which happens to equal 14, but all that matters is that we CAN solve for x. This means that we can solve for y, which equals 9, so the answer to the stem is YES. Sufficient.

120. (D)

The total income for the three years was (3)(45,000) = $135,000.

Let x represent the scientist's income the first year. Then the second-year income was $\frac{3}{2}x$ and the third-year income was $\frac{5}{2}x$. Therefore, $x + \frac{3}{2}x + \frac{5}{2}x = 135{,}000 \rightarrow 5x = 135{,}000 \rightarrow x = 27{,}000$. Thus, the second-year income was $\frac{3}{2}(27{,}000) = \$40{,}500$. The answer is D.

121. **(D)**

For a whole number n to have a remainder of 1 when divided by both 10 and 6, n – 1 must be divisible by both 10 and 6, or by the least common multiple of 10 and 6, which is 30. Therefore, the two-digit whole numbers that yield a remainder of 1 when divided by both 6 and 10 are multiples of 30, plus 1: 31, 61, and 91. There are only three such numbers. Thus, the answer is D.

122. **(A)**

First, multiply both sides of the equation by the least common denominator, 4y:

$4y\left(\frac{x^2 - 9}{2y}\right) = 4y\left(\frac{x-3}{4}\right)$, and $2(x^2 - 9) = y(x - 3)$. Then, express $x^2 - 9$ as $(x + 3)(x - 3)$ and divide both sides by x – 3: $\frac{2(x + 3)(x - 3)}{x - 3} = \frac{y(x - 3)}{x - 3} \rightarrow 2(x + 3) = y \rightarrow 2x + 6 = y \rightarrow 2x = y - 6 \rightarrow$ $x = \frac{y - 6}{2}$. Thus, the answer is A.

123. **(E)**

(1) We can't solve a two-variable system with only one equation. Insufficient.

(2) As with Statement 1, we can't solve a two-variable equation with only one equation. Insufficient. Together, one might be tempted to say that we have two equations, and thus enough to solve for the two variables. However, upon close inspection, you'll see that the two equations are identical, something to be on the watch for in many Data Sufficiency problems. The first equation "becomes" the second after you multiply each term by 6 and isolate the y term. This means that we still only have one equation. Insufficient.

124. **(B)**

$\frac{11}{23}$ and $\frac{7}{13}$ are each multiplied by x. Whatever the relationship between the two fractions, if x is a positive value, the relationship will stay the same. If x is negative, the relationship is reversed. NOTE: As it turns out, $\frac{11}{23}$ is a little less than $\frac{1}{2}$ (which equals $\frac{11}{22}$), and $\frac{7}{13}$ is just a little greater than $\frac{1}{2}$ (which equals $\frac{7}{14}$). This information, however, is not needed to solve the problem. (1) This tells us very little. If x is positive, then the answer to the stem is YES. If x is negative, the answer is NO. Insufficient. (2) This statement tells us that x is positive, so we will always get a YES in answer to the stem. Sufficient.

125. (B)

The least possible product in this case is the negative product having greatest absolute value, which can be obtained by multiplying the negative number with the greatest absolute value with the 3 greatest integers: $(-5) \cdot 10 \cdot 9 \cdot 8 = -3{,}600$. Thus, the answer is B.

126. (D)

Since distance equals rate times time, $D = rt$, where D, r, and t are the actual distance, rate, and time traveled. If the motorist drives 1 hour longer and at a rate 5 mph faster, the new distance $D_I = (r + 5)(t + 1) = rt + 70 \rightarrow rt + 5t + r + 5 = rt + 70 \rightarrow 5t + r = 65$

If instead, he drives 2 hours longer, and at a rate 10 mph faster, the new distance

$D_{II} = (r + 10)(t + 2) = rt + 1 - t + 2r + 20 = rt + 2(5t + r) + 20.$

Then, $D_{II} - D = [rt + 2(5t + r) + 20] - [rt] = 2(65) + 20 = 150$

The answer is therefore D.

127. (A)

The left hand side of the inequality can be expressed as $\dfrac{\frac{x}{2z} - y}{2z + \frac{z}{2z}}$, which can be further simplified to $\frac{x}{2z} - \frac{y}{2z} + \frac{1}{2}$. Now the question in the stem looks like this:

is $\frac{x}{2z} - \frac{y}{2z} + \frac{1}{2} < \frac{x}{2z} - \frac{y}{2z} - \frac{x}{y}$? Since the first two terms are the same on both sides, the real question is: is $\frac{1}{2} < -\frac{x}{y}$?

(1) Once we've simplified the inequality (done above), this statement tells us that the

answer to the question stem is YES. Sufficient.

(2) This tells us that the two unknowns have opposite signs: one is negative, one is positive. This means that $\frac{x}{y}$ is positive, but we don't know if it is larger than $\frac{1}{2}$. Insufficient.

128. (A)

If we use a common denominator of 12, the question reads:

Is $\frac{(20x - 8) - (15x - 3)}{12} > 0$? This simplifies to: Is $\frac{5x - 5}{12} > 0$? Multiplying each side of this by 12, and then adding 5 to each side, we get: is $5x > 5$? This can be further simplified to: is $x > 1$? (1) Once we've simplified the equation, this answers the question directly: YES. Sufficient. (2) This tells us that x must be positive (remember, we were told that it wasn't 0), but it could be a number between 0 and 1, (or it could be 1), thus giving us a NO, or it could be greater than 1, giving us a YES. Insufficient.

129. (C)

(1) This only tells us that – 7 is in the set. Insufficient. (2) This only tells us that 13 is in the set. Insufficient. Together, we know that the average of the set is also the average of – 7 and 13, which happens to be 3. When dealing with a set of consecutive numbers, the average of all the numbers is also the average of the first and last numbers, as well as the second and second-to-last numbers, etc. -- in other words, the average of the set is also the average of the nth smallest and nth largest numbers. Sufficient.

NOTE: Consecutively spaced numbers could be 1, 4, 7, 10, 13, etc. This doesn't necessarily have to mean 1, 2, 3, etc.

130. (A)

If you know how many <u>prime</u> factors a number has, you can then determine how many factors it has altogether. For example, knowing that the prime factors of 30 are 2, 3, and 5, you can derive all the other factors by multiplying the primes in every combination possible: $(2 \cdot 3)$, $(2 \cdot 5)$, $(3 \cdot 5)$, and $(2 \cdot 3 \cdot 5)$. Those four products AND the three primes themselves, AND 1 (always a factor) give us a total of 8 factors.

NOTE: "Distinct" means different: $x \neq y \neq z$.

(1) The question reads: how many positive factors does $(xy)^5$ have? The prime factorization of $(xy)^5$ is $(x \cdot y)(x \cdot y)(x \cdot y)(x \cdot y)(x \cdot y)$. Since x and y are primes, you can determine ALL the factors of $(xy)^5$ by multiplying the primes in every combination possible. The factors are: x, y, xy, x^2, y^2, x^2y, x^3y... x^5y^5 -- and of course, always 1. That's a lot of factors, but you don't need to count them up. All you need to know is that you <u>could</u> count them. Sufficient.

(2) This tells us nothing about z. We'll get different number of factors depending on the exponent we choose. Insufficient.

131. **(C)**

Let p be the price per ticket. Then if n tickets were sold, total revenues would be np. Let c be the total cost of the production. Then, if np is 20 percent greater than c, $np = 1.2c$. Since only 95 percent of the n tickets were sold, $0.95(np) = 0.95 (1.2c) = 1.14c$. Therefore, the total revenue from ticket sales was 14 percent greater than the total cost of production. Thus, the answer is C.

132. **(D)**

If the integer n has a remainder of 3 when it is divided by 6, then n is a number of the form $6q + 3$, where q is an integer. Therefore, $6q + 3$ can be substituted for n in each of the expressions listed until an expression is found that is not a multiple of 6 (does not have 6 as a factor). For example:

A) $n - 3 = (6q + 3) - 3 = 6q$;

B) $n + 3 = (6q + 3) + 3 = 6q + 6 = 6(q + 1)$;

C) $2n = 2(6q + 3) = 12q + 6 = 6(2q + 1)$;

D) $3n = 3(6q + 3) = 18q + 9 = 6(3q + 1) + 3$;

E) $4n = 4(6q + 3) = 24q + 12 = 6(4q + 2)$.

Since the expression given for choice D has a remainder of 3 when divided by 6, it is not

a multiple of 6. Alternatively, this problem can be approached by taking a number that satisfies the parameters of *n* and plugging it into the answer choices, e.g. 9, which, when divided by 6, has a remainder of 3.

A) $n - 3$: $9 - 3 = 6$, which is a multiple of 6

B) $n + 3$: $9 + 3 = 12$, which is a multiple of 6

C) $2n$: $2(9) = 18$, which is a multiple of 6

D) $3n$: $3(9) = 27$, which is NOT a multiple of 6

E) $4n$: $4(9) = 36$, which is a multiple of 6

Therefore, the answer is D.

133. **(C)**

If *x* is the number of liters of alcohol that must be added to a solution that already contains 20 liters of alcohol (20% of 100 liters), then $20 + x$ liters must be 25 percent of the total number of liters in the new solution, which will consist of $100 + x$ liters. Therefore, the equation to be solved is $20 + x = 0.25(100 + x)$. This reduces to $20 + x = 25 + 0.25x$, and $0.75x = 5$. The value of $x = \frac{5}{0.75} = \frac{20}{3}$. Thus, the answer is C.

134. **(D)**

Each of the 10 persons shakes hands 9 times, once with each of the other 9 people at the reunion. Since there are 10 people, each of whom shakes hands with the other 9 people, it would seem at first that there are 10(9) or 90 handshakes. However, since each handshake was counted twice, once for each of the two people involved, the correct number of handshakes is half of that: $\frac{90}{2}$, or 45. Alternatively, since this problem requires finding all combinations of 2 amidst a group of 10, a formula can be used: $_{10}C_2 = \frac{10!}{(10 - 2)! \cdot 2!} = \frac{10 \cdot 9}{2} = 45$. Thus, the answer is D.

Answer Key

Lesson

1 . . . . . . E
2 . . . . . . A
3 C
4 . . . . . . B
5 C
6 . . . . . . D
7 . . . . . . D
8 . . . . . . B
9 . . . . . . D
10 C
11 C
12 . . . . . A
13 . . . . . B
14 . . . . . E
15 C
16 . . . . . E
17 . . . . . A
18 . . . . . D
19 . . . . . B
20 . . . . . E

Assorted

21 . . . . . A
22 C
23 C
24 . . . . . D
25 . . . . . D
26 . . . . . D
27 . . . . . A
28 C
29 . . . . . A
30 . . . . . B
31 . . . . . B

32 . . . . . E
33 . . . . . A
34 . . . . . E
35 . . . . . B
36 C
37 . . . . . D
38 . . . . . D
39 C
40 . . . . . D
41 C
42 . . . . . B
43 . . . . . B
44 C
45 C
46 . . . . . D
47 . . . . . A
48 . . . . . A
49 C
50 . . . . . E
51 . . . . . E
52 . . . . . B
53 . . . . . D
54 . . . . . B
55 . . . . . E
56 . . . . . E
57 . . . . . E
58 . . . . . A
59 . . . . . D
60 C
61 . . . . . B
62 . . . . . D
63 C
64 . . . . . E
65 . . . . . E
66 . . . . . E
67 . . . . . B
68 . . . . . D
69 . . . . . D

70 . . . . . A
71 . . . . . E
72 C
73 . . . . . D
74 . . . . . A
75 . . . . . B
76 . . . . . E
77 C
78 . . . . . A
79 . . . . . A
80 . . . . . D
81 . . . . . E
82 . . . . . D
83 . . . . . E
84 . . . . . B
85 C
86 . . . . . E
87 . . . . . B
88 . . . . . A
89 . . . . . D
90 C
91 . . . . . B
92 C
93 . . . . . E
94 . . . . . E
95 . . . . . E
96 . . . . . D
97 . . . . . A
98 . . . . . B
99 . . . . . E
100 . . . . B
101 . . . . A
102 . . . . B
103 C
104 C
105 . . . . A
106 C
107 C

108 . . . . D
109 . . . . D
110 . . . . B
111 . . . . D
112 C
113 . . . . E
114 C

Challenge

115 . . . . D
116 C
117 C
118 . . . . A
119 . . . . D
120 . . . . D
121 . . . . D
122 . . . . A
123 . . . . E
124 . . . . B
125 . . . . B
126 . . . . D
127 . . . . A
128 . . . . A
129 C
130 . . . . A
131 C
132 . . . . D
133 C
134 . . . . D

THE MBA TOUR
Your future begins here

The MBA Tour offers Quality Interaction With Top Business Schools

MEET with school representatives at our OPEN FAIR

LISTEN to top school experts discuss valuable MBA admission topics at our PANEL PRESENTATIONS

DISCUSS individual school qualities with representatives at our ROUNDTABLE EVENTS

ASIA	UNITED STATES	SOUTH AMERICA	CANADA
TOKYO	HOUSTON	BUENOS AIRES	CALGARY
SEOUL	CHICAGO	SANTIAGO	VANCOUVER
TAIPEI	ATLANTA	SAO PAULO	TORONTO
BEIJING	NEW YORK	LIMA	MONTREAL
SHANGHAI	BOSTON	BOGOTA	
BANGKOK	WASHINGTON DC	MEXICO CITY	
SINGAPORE	LOS ANGELES		
	SAN FRANCISCO	EUROPE	
INDIA		MUNICH	
BANGALORE		LONDON	
NEW DELHI		PARIS	
MUMBAI			

Register at www.thembatour.com